Manchester
50 years of change

Manchester

50 years of change

Post-War planning in Manchester

London: HMSO

ISBN 0 11 702006 0

Front cover and frontispiece: St Ann's Square (Len Grant)
Cover and title page spread (background illustration): detail of aerial photograph of the city centre (Jefferson's)

Author and publisher have attempted, so far without success, to trace the copyright holder for the Hulme Consultations and Hulme Crescents photographs (by Bridget Soltau and Paul Herrmann respectively), which appear in chapter 9. If the legal copyright holders in question wish to contact HMSO, we shall ensure that the correct acknowledgement appears in any future edition of this book.

Published by HMSO and available from:

HMSO Publications Centre
(Mail, fax and telephone orders only)
PO Box 276, London SW8 5DT
Telephone orders 0171 873 9090
General enquiries 0171 873 0011
(queuing system in operation for both numbers)
Fax orders 0171 873 8200

HMSO Bookshops
49 High Holborn, London WC1V 6HB
(counter service only)
0171 873 0011 Fax 0171 831 1326
68–69 Bull Street, Birmingham B4 6AD
0121 236 9696 Fax 0121 236 9699
33 Wine Street, Bristol BS1 2BQ
0117 9264306 Fax 0117 9294515
9–21 Princess Street, Manchester M60 8AS
0161 834 7201 Fax 0161 833 0634
16 Arthur Street, Belfast BT1 4GD
01232 238451 Fax 01232 235401
71 Lothian Road, Edinburgh EH3 9AZ
0131 228 4181 Fax 0131 229 2734
The HMSO Oriel Bookshop
The Friary, Cardiff CF1 4AA
01222 395548 Fax 01222 384347

HMSO's Accredited Agents
(see Yellow Pages)

and through good booksellers

Contents

Preface

Being born and bred in Manchester, a true Mancunian, I have witnessed many of the changes that have taken place throughout the City. I was born and raised in Collyhurst where rows upon rows of densely packed terraced houses led to poor living conditions. I can still remember when the Manchester streets were lit by gaslights and smog created from coal fires provided adventure for a child of my age. Unfortunately, the smog killed many people and it was obvious that something needed to be done to change the conditions experienced by Manchester people.

In 1938 I moved away from the Collyhurst area to what I thought of as a palace in Blackley with an inside toilet and bath. The area where I was born was demolished in an attempt to dramatically improve living conditions. The following years were dominated by World War Two and I remember vividly the mass destruction that the German Bombers brought, especially over the Christmas period of 1940. A great many City Centre buildings and landmarks were destroyed and much effort was put into rebuilding the City after the war had ended.

During the 1960's, housing was constructed at a rapid rate, partly to replace the homes damaged during the war and partly to rehouse those people affected by the slum clearance programme. Unfortunately, the high rise developments that replaced the slums and the overspill estates that housed many of the City's residents were, with hindsight, unacceptable. I am pleased that we are now getting to grips with these problems and with close consultation with local residents we hope to provide high quality homes and environments that will serve the citizens of Manchester well.

The role of the tram has come full circle during my lifetime and from the last tram car in Manchester in 1949 with Metrolink we now have the makings of a transport system of the future. Although at present the coverage is limited, with new developments on the horizon we might yet have a comprehensive network of tramways that will help provide an answer to the problems of traffic and pollution.

We now know the outcome of Manchester's bid to become the host City for the 2002 Commonwealth Games. I hope that with the Velodrome, Manchester Arena and proposed Millennium Stadium, Manchester can become a centre for sporting excellence.

I firmly believe that with the changes that have occurred in the City recently and the proposals that we are currently pursuing, we are heading for a better Manchester. For older readers this book will trigger many memories of how Manchester used to be and just how much it has changed. For younger people it should prove to be an invaluable lesson in a great City's recent history.

N. Franklin

Ken Franklin

Chair, Environmental Planning Committee

November 1995

Introduction

We are very careless with our contemporary history. Manchester, like many cities, has seen major changes take place in the post-war period when formal and powerful planning legislation has been in place, and these changes in their own ways may well have been as profound in their impact on the City as the changes that have taken place in any other 50 year period, with the possible exception of the time of the height of the Industrial Revolution. Yet this is a story that to date has been poorly told. The exhibition of 50 years of planning experience in Manchester, and this book that accompanies it, set out to begin to redress this balance; and the associated decision to establish and maintain a planning archive in Manchester ought to ensure that the story can be better told in future.

This is not to say that nothing has been done. For example, in recent times the decisions of various parties to commission the local photographer Len Grant to record on a systematic basis the major changes that have been taking place on the Lower Mosley Street site where the new Concert Hall is being constructed and at Victoria Station where the new arena (now known as the Nynex Arena) has been built were important steps forward. The photographics record they have already produced tells in each case a fascinating story of parts of the City's history in the making, and we would be the poorer had this not been done. As yet, however, these are isolated examples; we need this approach to become a more standard feature of the management of major changes in our great cities.

The real point of all this is that the story of the planning era is simply another period in the life of our cities. It is a story that deserves to be told, therefore, just as much as the stories of those other eras deserve to be told. It is a story that is shaping tomorrow's city as we speak; that often attracts considerable controversy and countervailing sets of opinions; but that above all is reflective of a process that is almost certainly here to stay in one form or another. The need for effective city planning is now established throughout most of the world; the real question is no longer whether we have planning in our great cities, but rather how well are we doing it and how can we improve it. People cannot really have views about these sorts of things unless they have some knowledge of what is being attempted through the planning process. Above all, therefore, the purpose of this book and of the accompanying exhibition is to begin to tell the story of 50 years of post-war planning activity in Manchester as neutrally as possible. The intent is neither to glorify its success nor to whitewash its failures; it is simply to tell the story as it is, so that people can make up their own minds about these sorts of matters if they wish, or can merely absorb that story as part of the city's history if that is what they wish.

We are very pleased that this project has come to fruition, because we need to remember our history in everything we do. We hope that people reading this book feel better informed about Manchester's planning history, and perhaps feel better able as a consequence to understand the historic forces that are helping to shape what we are doing today. If these objectives can be achieved the project will be well worthwhile.

Acknowledgements

In compiling this record of the history of planning in Manchester over the last 50 years the Council has reason to thank a great many people without whom the task would have been impossible. Firstly, thanks go to all the City Planning Officers to head the Department since its inception in 1965; John Millar, Brian Parnell, Ted Kitchen and David Kaiserman. Secondly, thanks to all the officers that currently work in the Department who contributed to the process. Thanks also go to Robert Maund, Chris Makepeace, David Rudlin, Pam Bishop and Penny Boothman. In providing an overall editorial role the Council wishes to thank the University of Manchester Department of Planning and Landscape for their involvement.

Finally special thanks go to HMSO who put time, effort and dedication into producing the document in a very short timescale. Also special thanks to the Co-op Bank who sponsored the public exhibition that is associated with the book and without whose support the project may never have gone ahead.

Phill Bamford
Project Co-ordinator 1995

1 Manchester and the Industrial Revolution

Although Manchester has pre-Roman origins the development of the town began in 79AD when troops from the Roman Army established a turf and timber fort in the area, as an intermediate post between York and Chester, Buxton and Ribchester. The site chosen lay at the junction of the River Medlock and River Irwell and gave the fort natural protection on two sides. Around 200AD the fort was expanded and replaced by a stone structure that could accommodate around 500 men, but it was abandoned in 410AD when the Romans left the country.

During the medieval period the town's development was pursued at the more northerly confluence of the Irk and Irwell around the area of the present cathedral. By the eighteenth century the township began to expand southwards, whilst the building of the Bridgewater Canal stimulated the development of the area where the ruined Roman fort lay in open fields. So the castle in the field became known as 'Castlefield'. These two areas expanded towards each other and by 1878, when the Town Hall was constructed in Albert Square, much of the area was built up.

During the eighteenth century South East Lancashire was predominantly an agricultural area with Manchester a market town at its centre. This was soon to change as the demand for cotton soared during the latter part of the century. With the climatic advantages that the area experienced – high humidity, high rainfall and an abundance of soft water – Manchester became the

The River Irwell in the mid-19th Century lined with warehouses and factories during the 1800's. Victoria Bridge is depicted which was opened in 1839 built at a cost of £20,000.

2   *Manchester: 50 years of change*

Opposite: Constructed in 1851 by S & J Watts the Watts Warehouse was a multi-storey building with each floor reflecting a different architectural style. This picture was taken in the 1860's.

Above: Construction work being carried out on the Manchester Ship Canal which opened on 1st January 1894.

focus of attention for the cotton industry and a dramatic increase in mill building ensued over the next 50 years. Indeed its population grew over fourfold from 76,000 in 1801 to 316,000 in 1851.

The transport developments that occurred in the region during this period further enhanced the economic position of Manchester. During the 1760's, the Duke of Bridgewater constructed what is thought to be the country's first cut canal, to link his coal mine in Worsley with the market in Manchester, at a cost of £220,000. This led to the subsequent development of a great network of waterways.

With this boom in canal building the mills in Manchester began to expand rapidly. As the price of land in the town centre rose fast, mills began to locate in edge of town areas such as Ancoats and Chorlton-on-Medlock. Through this expansion, Manchester became the largest and most highly concentrated centre of cotton manufacture and distribution in the world. Many other industries developed in the City and surrounding towns but almost all were derived from cotton. The chemical industry developed from the bleaching and dyeing of cotton goods and engineering from the need to build and repair cotton machinery.

Another major development in Manchester's transport history was the construction of the world's first public passenger railway station. After trials held at Rainhill, won by 'Stephenson's Rocket', the inaugural trip from Manchester to Liverpool was undertaken on 15 September 1830. The railway was an enormous success, covering the 31 mile journey in under two hours and carrying over half a million passengers in its first full year.

Manchester City Council came into being in 1853 after the incorporation of several surrounding townships in 1838. There was a desperate need for a competent authority to deal with the economic and social problems created by the rapid expansion of the area during the Industrial Revolution. Its remit was to improve the quality of life for those who lived and worked in the City, a goal which has been pursued ever since.

From around 1853 the mills began to decline in the centre of the City. The price of land was becoming too expensive and competition for space was increasing. Mills continued to be built in areas like Ancoats and in the towns surrounding the City, and warehouses were still built in the centre during this period. Perhaps the most elegant of all was constructed in 1851 by S. and J. Watts who created a multi-storey warehouse with each floor designed in a different architectural style – Egyptian, Dutch, Italian and Elizabethan; in 1982 this building was converted into the Britannia Hotel at a cost of £5 million.

Reproduced by kind permission of the Local History Library

By the 1870's Britain was facing increasing competition from businesses in Germany and the United States. Manchester, as the centre of the cotton industry in Britain, proposed a radical solution to the problem in order to make itself more competitive. The plan was to join Manchester directly to the open sea via a huge canal that would avoid the need for costly rail transport and dock charges at Liverpool. Under the leadership of Daniel Adamson this idea was transformed into reality and in 1885 the Ship Canal Bill was passed by Parliament allowing construction to begin. The official business opening of the canal came on New Year's Day 1894 and although at first it ran at a loss, it allowed the haulage of heavy freight and made it possible for Manchester to become a centre for engineering.

The cotton era has left a significant legacy of buildings in the Greater Manchester area and it is the Victorian and Edwardian structure that still dominates the City today. The cotton warehouses were not just practical buildings but ornate palaces designed for merchant princes. Both mills and warehouses remain a dominant presence in the urban landscape of Manchester and present a constant reminder of a former way of working and living. As well as telling us much about the working conditions of previous generations, both building types were often impressive and state-of-the-art with their own individual style and character, covering a wide variety of dates and architectural type. This irreplaceable

A sketch of Manchester City Centre by W. Randolph in 1892. The cathedral can clearly be seen at the centre of the picture with Victoria Bridge (left) and Blackfriars Bridge (right).

part of our industrial history is under constant threat.

The growth of Manchester's financial sector stemmed directly from its industrial growth and has left a legacy of buildings in the City; for example, the Royal Bank of Scotland (formerly the Manchester and Salford Bank) on Mosley Street constructed in 1862. It has also given Manchester a range of activities both commercial and industrial that are important to this day in its role of the 'Regional Centre'.

The road layout, the architectural form of buildings and the main streets and spaces were all determined in the Victorian and Edwardian periods when the City was rising to international stature. It is not surprising then that the present City is still dominated by the physical forms from that time.

Until the end of the nineteenth century, the provision of housing of all kinds was the sole responsibility of private enterprise. A few enlightened social reformers set out to provide housing in Manchester which was cheap and of a reasonable quality, but most of the housing was designed to minimum standards. Partly as a result of initiatives taken by Manchester Corporation, Acts of Parliament were passed to govern both design and layout of housing and this led to a change in the way the development of the City was regulated.

2 The Early Planning Effort

During the Industrial Revolution the population of Manchester rose at an alarming rate. There was no formal means of controlling this expansion at the time and buildings were erected unregulated. Before 1868 there were no construction by-laws and speculative builders could cram many houses onto a site with no restrictions as to light, air or room space. Until 1890 damp courses were not required. Not surprisingly most houses were damp, dingy and drab.

With people moving into the area faster than the authorities could handle, properties that would normally have been condemned were left standing. New property was built as quickly and cheaply as possible. The population of Manchester rose dramatically from 544,000 in 1901 to 766,000 in 1931. This influx of people created a great number of slum areas with high densities,

poor living and health conditions and a lack of sanitary facilities.

The story of municipal housing in Manchester dates back to 1891. At that time, new housing and public health by-laws were leading to the demolition of substandard dwellings but Manchester's population was still on the increase creating an acute lack of affordable housing. The first municipal housing schemes took place on Oldham Road and Pollard Street. Similar projects were completed along Rochdale Road in 1904, comprising blocks of flats five stories high, arranged in the form of a square around a central open space covered with asphalt and used as a children's playground. They represented a big improvement in standards of accommodation.

A few years later a small suburban housing development was built in Burnage. Five miles south of the City Centre, it followed many of the principles of the Garden Village movement promoted by Ebenezer Howard and became known as Burnage Garden Village. The 11 acre site off Burnage Lane was purchased from Earl Egerton of Tatton in 1907 and the underlying concept was to ensure that every house was so placed as to have the maximum amount of light, air and pleasant outlook as possible. The development comprised 136 houses constructed around a circular road pattern at a density of 12 dwellings per acre. Grass verges and tree-lined avenues reinforced the garden village atmosphere and tennis courts and a bowling green were also provided. The design was all part of an experiment to promote social interaction between the tenants. Every house was supplied with hot and cold running water as well as electricity which, at the time, was a major step forward, especially for rented accommodation. The major drawback of this development was that it did little to re-house the poor from slum areas. The quality of construction meant that rental levels were set too high for the working classes to afford. However, it did provide a model for future estate development in the Manchester area.

A private development along similar lines was completed at Chorltonville in 1911. On 40 acres of attractive land to the south side of Chorlton-cum-Hardy, an estate of 273 houses was built at a cost in excess of £100,000. Each pair of houses differed in design from its neighbour both internally and externally. Open spaces were also planned with $5\frac{1}{2}$ acres of land set aside for recreation. The opening ceremony took place on 7 October 1911 and the development was a huge success. It received many commendations including the following:

> The village is another attempt to solve the housing problem of a great city, and the effect of their broad grass verges, and the broken

This shows the 'Gibraltar' area off Red Bank near the River Irk. The premises built in 1668 were in their final stages of decay.

One of the first municipal housing schemes was completed around 1904 at Victoria Court in the Rochdale Road area.

outline of the villas, with their prominent black and white gables and expansive bay windows is very pleasing. Light, sunshine and fresh air have been the main considerations in the erection of the houses. (*Manchester Evening Chronicle*, 7 October 1911)

The garden suburb idea has been put into operation in many parts of the country but nowhere with more outstanding success than at Chorltonville. (*Manchester Evening Chronicle*, 21 October 1911)

In 1918, in attempting to prepare a plan for south Manchester, it was decided that widescale consultation was needed between the various authorities. As a consequence the Manchester and District Joint Town Planning Advisory Committee was founded in 1920, responsible for all areas within a 15 mile radius of the Town Hall. In 1922 an exhibition and conference on town planning was successfully staged by the Committee at Manchester's Town Hall. As the need to prepare land use plans became apparent, the Advisory Committee recommended the setting up of 15 separate town planning committees each responsible for its own area.

Between 1927 and 1929 the Manchester Corporation achieved an average building rate of nearly 2,500 houses a year, but this rapid growth created a new problem for the City. Suitable sites were in short supply and therefore a new solution had to be found.

On 3 May 1926 Manchester City Council purchased 4,000 acres of the Tatton Estate surrounding Wythenshawe Hall in North Cheshire. The corporation appointed a nationally known town planner, Barry Parker, as a consultant to begin the development of a major new housing estate to rehouse people affected by the inner city slum clearance programme. Until the outbreak of World War II construction proceeded to a design which was undoubtedly ahead of its time. The plan was to create a satellite town with areas set aside for housing, agriculture, parks and open spaces, shopping centres, community facilities and industry. These developments were serviced by a network of tree-lined roads and parkways. The land lay within the boundary of Bucklow Rural District Council and as a consequence Manchester had no control over town planning in the area. Therefore, Manchester decided to apply to Parliament to extend the City's boundary. This

was something which they did not achieve until the Manchester Extension Act 1930, when Wythenshawe became the country's first municipally owned satellite town.

Over the first ten years dwellings were constructed at a rapid rate and by 1935 the local population had reached 35,000. During the war years however, development took a back seat as public money was diverted into the war effort. After the war expansion plans progressed rapidly in the knowledge that the Wythenshawe area would accommodate the City's first, second and third-year post-war housing programmes. The desperate need for new housing led to the construction of predominantly residential units and industrial estates. Unfortunately, the provision of social facilities fell short of what had originally been envisaged.

Wythenshawe satellite town designed as a self-contained area with houses, industry, shops and social facilities to rehouse people from the inner city.

A celebration of the 50th Anniversary of Burnage Garden Village. Completed in 1906 the development of 136 houses followed the principles of the Garden Village movement.

By 1964 the original goal of 100,000 population had been reached but the relentless pressure for development of houses had left an estate barren of basic amenities. Wythenshawe's misfortune was that because construction straddled one world war and a great depression it was never developed to its full potential.

3 World War II and the Effects of Bombing

On 3 September 1939 World War II broke out and no-one could have envisaged the destruction that this would bring to Manchester. It was not until 20 June 1940 that people had to enter their shelters as the first air-raid sirens sounded over the City. Although the sounds of aircraft could be heard on this day, no bombs were actually dropped and Manchester was left to hold its breath with the thought that it might have been a reconnaissance mission. German aircraft were not seen again for some five weeks, but on the 29 August 1940 they returned to drop the first bombs on the Manchester area. Relatively little damage was caused but this good fortune was not to last for much longer.

On two consecutive fateful nights in December, Manchester was to receive its heaviest bombing raids of the war. The nights of 22nd and 23rd saw the Christmas Blitz, as it became known, bringing devastation to the City.

The siren sounded at 6.38 pm on the 22nd and two minutes later an incendiary fell in the Albert Square area. After this, bombs and incendiaries were dropped all over the City Centre bringing fire and destruction. A building in Princess Street was hit and part of the Victoria Buildings on Deansgate collapsed into the road, blocking the thoroughfare from Blackfriars Bridge to Victoria Bridge. The raid lasted five hours and in that time 233 high explosive bombs were dropped on the City, together with many more incendiary

On the night of 22nd December 1940 the Free Trade Hall was completely destroyed.

devices. The fires that raged throughout the night were all under control by 11.30 am the next morning, but this was only a taste of what was to come.

The following night at 7.14 pm sirens signalled the beginning of another Luftwaffe air raid. This time the attack lasted over six hours and although only 55 high explosive bombs were dropped the devastation was even more acute than on the previous night. One of the reasons for this destruction was that a strong north-easterly wind blew up at 3 am, spreading the already blazing fires from building to building. There were 1,300 fires in Manchester and from the surrounding areas it appeared as if the whole City Centre was alight. The Piccadilly area was a mass of flames and the already overstretched fire services were unable to contain the inferno. By dawn fires had spread to Portland Street and a decision was taken to call in the Royal Engineers to dynamite the buildings to create a fire break. Charges were laid and several buildings were purposely destroyed in order to successfully contain the spread of the fire.

The death toll in Manchester over the two night raids came to 363 with a further 455 seriously injured. Almost 10 acres of land in the City was destroyed and areas such as Market Place and Piccadilly were devastated. Many notable buildings were also damaged throughout the raids including parts of the Cathedral, the Coal Exchange and a newly opened private ward at the Manchester Eye Hospital. The Free Trade Hall was reduced to a shell when a high explosive scored a direct hit. Platform 16 of Manchester's Victoria Station also suffered significant damage.

During the two-day blitz nearly 30,000 houses were damaged and many people were rendered

Below: Parker Street, another area of severe bomb damage.

Opposite: Twisted metal and rubble along part of Cannon Street following the Manchester Blitz.

Devastation as the two day Manchester Blitz destroyed almost 10 acres of land in the City Centre.

homeless. Manchester Corporation reacted quickly and by 2 January 1941 approximately 13,000 houses had received emergency repairs.

But in the midst of adversity there is always hope. The Lord Mayor of Manchester, Leonard B. Cox, looked to the future and produced a statement entitled, 'We Plan a Fairer City'. He believed that post-war reconstruction should seek to rectify the errors of the past and help to solve the City's housing crisis. He announced plans for the complete elimination of slum dwellings, replacing them with comfortable and well-planned homes. He also recognised that the reconstruction of war-damaged areas presented an opportunity. Parts of the City could be replanned to create new open spaces incorporating wider streets, dignified buildings and ample squares, green spaces and tree-bordered avenues.

Although the war had brought destruction to much of the City's central area, the future for Manchester looked bright.

Destruction brought by the bombings to residential areas. During the two day Blitz nearly 30,000 houses were damaged in the Manchester area.

4 The City of Manchester Plan 1945

In 1941 Lord Reith, when addressing a regional forum, advised Manchester City Council to prepare a provisional plan for redevelopment. He suggested that those responsible for planning in Manchester 'should not consider themselves bound by existing legislation, but they should plan boldly and comprehensively.'

Towards the end of World War II it became apparent that extensive rebuilding would need to be carried out throughout the whole of the Manchester area. Damage caused during the bombing raids had to be rectified and major problems relating to living and working conditions needed to be solved.

Therefore, in 1945 the City Council produced its first ever comprehensive plan for the Manchester area prepared by Roland Nicholas, the City's Chief Surveyor and Engineer. It was envisaged that 'If every stage of this process of reconstruction is made to conform with the master plan the Manchester of 50 years hence will be a City transformed.'

The Nicholas Plan was dominated by a desire to start afresh. There was an attempt to remove all traces of Victorian Manchester because of its links with poor living, working and health conditions, and to replace it with 'modern mechanisms' to run an international city. This would be reflected in new road patterns and an international style of building.

Housing

The problem of overcrowding in the inner city areas of Manchester was acute after the war years and in order to achieve a decent standard of living in these localities it was believed that the population had to be reduced by over half.

Even after the programme of slum clearance during the pre-war years, Manchester still had around 68,000 houses described as unfit for human habitation by the Medical Officer of Health. Most of these were in areas where the density was over 24 dwellings per acre. Therefore the plan prescribed a series of density standards much lower than had previously been allowed in order to avoid building slums of the future in redeveloped areas.

New neighbourhoods were to be created in outlying areas in order to accommodate displaced

An artist's impression (1945) of the proposed boulevard leading to Albert Square and the new Town Hall. The existing Town Hall Extension and Central Library can be seen to the right.

people. They would be designed to supply the immediate needs of everyday living and be self-contained in order to foster a sense of place and interest in community life. The ideal size of such neighbourhoods would be a population of 10,000 which would therefore easily support churches, shops, playing fields, schools and public houses as well as a community centre, health centre and branch library.

A cluster of neighbourhoods would form a District with a population of around 50,000. Each district would support a wider range of facilities such as a main health centre, cinemas, public baths, police and fire stations and other social provisions. One such district, and easily the largest, was to be Wythenshawe.

Transport

The problems associated with the motor vehicle were already being felt by the City in the 1940s and an extensive study concluded that cross-town traffic must be removed from the City Centre. To bring this about, four new ring roads were proposed by the Council – an Outer, Intermediate and Inner Ring Road as well as a City Circle

Road. These highways would enable long-distance and suburban traffic to pass through the City quickly and avoid the City Centre. Other proposals to ease the flow of traffic into Manchester were also considered with the extension of radial routes to intersect with the new ring roads making a spider's web of communication lines. An underground railway system was also considered to ease the flow of daily traffic into the centre, an idea first put forward in 1902.

There was also a need to revitalise the Deansgate area of the City and replan the heavily bombed parts between Manchester and Salford. The plan proposed the construction of a new railway and bus terminus (referred to as 'Trinity Station') to be sited between the existing Salford and Exchange Stations. It would replace and combine main-line services from Victoria, Exchange, Salford and Central stations allowing the through running of trains from Liverpool to Hull. Piccadilly Station (then called London Road) was to have been moved nearer to Piccadilly Gardens.

During this period air travel was just beginning and the plan states that 'Of all the prophecies which a planner is called upon to make none is more hazardous than to predict the future of air transport.' Nonetheless, Ringway was seen as a key development in the growth of Manchester. Air travel was so new that American journals were discussing the possibility of the auto-aircraft, a car with wings, and the plan itself stated that 'We may have to reckon with an extensive use of airliners with air taxis stationed on flat roofed buildings and folding winged autoplanes housed in private garages.' Manchester City Council felt that Ringway should become one of the country's major airports, recording that 'it may be as vital to the City in this century as was the building of the Ship Canal in the last.'

The Environment

In common with other northern towns the centre of Manchester was developed at a time when land was considered to be too valuable to be wasted on parks and gardens. As a consequence there was hardly any open space in the City Centre and the plan sought to rectify this situation.

In the inner city, special playgrounds were to be created for young children with sand gardens, paddling pools and swings and slides. Also, in areas of new development, open spaces were to be linked by field paths making it possible to walk through a neighbourhood without using the road system.

Another major aim of the plan was to deal with the problem of smoke pollution in the City. Atmospheric pollution was seen as the greatest

An artist's impression (1945) of the possible future development of Ringway.

Proposed in the 1945 Plan, a Cultural Centre on Oxford Road would have provided a Concert Hall and the City Assembly.

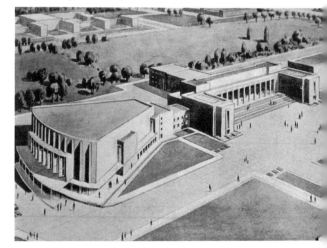

Proposal for Cathedral An impression of the Cathedral and surroundings as proposed in the 1945 Plan. The gardens in the foreground extend over the River Irwell.

enemy to public health and the target was the complete elimination of this problem.

The City Centre

The proposals for redesigning the City Centre were extensive and a summary of the key features are as follows:

The Cathedral was to be restored after its war damage and set in formal gardens linking it with Chetham's School, therefore creating a spacious precinct. The Law Courts and Town Hall areas were to be linked with a tree-lined boulevard. Brazenose Street still shows some of the elements of the plan. The extensive clearance of the Piccadilly area caused by the bombings led to proposals for an amusement centre incorporating a cinema, a skating rink, a boxing stadium, restaurants and other entertainment facilities. These would be linked with a comprehensive scheme to develop the gardens with a fountain, floodlights and trees festooned with coloured lights.

The proposals contained within the 1945 Plan were the ideas of Roland Nicholas. At the time, his vision was considered to be remarkable for its depth of research, its commitment to producing a human scale environment and its detailed incorporation of contemporary planning concepts. At the national level much attention was being devoted to the creation of the New Town Programme and in many ways the 1945 Plan for Manchester was a reflection of the New Town zeal.

Many of the proposals in the plan were not implemented because of the massive costs involved in the comprehensive clearance and redevelopment. Had they been followed, as Nicholas had envisaged, many of the City's landmarks, such as the Town Hall, would have been lost. Other proposals including the redevelopment of inner city housing areas such as Miles Platting, Beswick and Collyhurst did go ahead.

5 The 1961 Development Plan

The purpose of the 1961 Development Plan was to give a broad indication of the Council's intentions relating to the future use of land within the City's boundaries. It outlined development that was expected to take place during the plan period and also included long-term proposals in key areas such as roads and estate development. The plan itself covered 14 main subject areas: housing, shopping, education, open space, industry, the City Centre, minerals, roads, communications, tree planting, public utilities, university, cultural areas and health.

The Housing Acts of the time allowed for the clearance of slum dwellings and this was complemented by Compulsory Purchase Order powers, backed up by the 1961 Plan, to allow comprehensive redevelopment to take place. The plan period was designed to cover the ten years between 1961 and 1971, during which a total of 23,320 new dwellings were proposed to be built within the City boundary. In addition to this a further 32,480 dwellings were to be constructed outside the Manchester City Council area on overspill estates in Lancashire, Cheshire and Derbyshire. Therefore a total of 55,800 dwelling houses were to be constructed over the life of the

plan – an ambitious target but one that was necessary in order to ensure the clearance of slum dwellings. In order to reduce housing densities within the areas of redevelopment, the 1961 plan prescribed a net density of 90 habitable rooms per acre, a reduction in some areas of 30 per cent.

Retail developments were proposed in the plan in the new town areas of Wythenshawe, Blackley and Charlestown as well as further educational provision. Although no specific sites were identified, open space was to be made available in all renewal areas and in new developments at a standard of not less than 1.2 acres per 1,000 population.

Within the central area of the City the bulk of the development would be concentrated on the rebuilding of war-damaged areas. These included Strangeways, Market Place, Water Street, Swan Street, Shudehill, Piccadilly, Portland Street, Oxford Street and Faulkner Street.

The road programme during this period was extensive and proposals for a City Centre Road as well as three new ring roads (Inner, Intermediate and Outer) as proposed by the 1945 Plan were again highlighted. Extensive works were planned to the main radial roads that carried traffic into the City and the formation of a network of main

Left: Wythenshawe Civic Centre built in the 1960's conforming almost exactly to the original design as shown on the right.

roads and motorway-style intersections was the ultimate goal. Although the plan stated that around 1,150 properties would have to be demolished for the road proposals to go ahead, the actual figure would have been far greater.

For the university areas the Town Map highlighted sites to be reserved for the expansion of the educational facilities at the Victoria University of Manchester. The Council stated its intention to work closely with the university authorities in order to secure the development of a University Precinct.

The 1961 plan is short in length and very general in its approach to setting out the future development of the City. However, it was a key document in the history of the planning of the City mostly confirming existing land-uses. In many ways it was grounded in the Nicholas Plan of 1945 and updated to take account of the 1947 Town and Country Planning Act. Although submitted to the Secretary of State in 1951, it was not approved until 1961 when it was already ten years out of date. Therefore, although intended to cover a ten-year period, the plan fell into disuse long before it was superseded by the 1995 Manchester Plan, formally adopted on 21 July 1995.

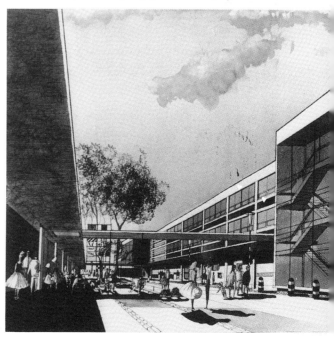

Stuart Street   A tiny property at Stuart Street, Bradford showing the quality of housing accommodation before redevelopment.

6 The Post-War Housing Problem and Solutions

The outbreak of World War II effectively brought a halt to large-scale redevelopment, but the City remained in desperate need of housing. In response, thousands of temporary prefabricated bungalows were provided in an attempt to alleviate the problem. They were built on very small sites and eventually on the edge of civic parks because there was never any intention that they should become a long-term solution to the problem. In the event some lasted for 30 years.

It was not until 1954, when new legislation allowed the Corporation to continue its slum clearance programme, that Manchester's bright new start could begin. Before this period, much of the City's efforts had been spent on repairing war damage and because of a lack of powers and resources, it was not until 1955 that significant progress could be made. By this time around

Above: An example of the inner city redevelopment and rehousing problems which faced the City after the war.

Below: Large scale clearance of unfit dwellings during the period of post-war redevelopment.

70,000 dwellings had been declared unfit for human habitation. As a first step a five-year programme of clearance was drawn up including the demolition of 7,500 properties. In the event the council fell 1,000 short of its target and it became clear that a more ambitious approach was necessary. Therefore, from 1960 onwards, the clearance programme was greatly expanded and the first four areas to be chosen were Hulme, Beswick, Longsight and Harpurhey.

In clearance areas both high- and low-rise dwellings were built to replace the previous slums. The approach usually began with a series of Compulsory Purchase Orders to transfer ownership to the Council before demolition. The new lower density schemes provided areas of open space, a commodity that had been drastically lacking in the slum areas of the inner city. Rapid development reduced population levels by as much as 50 per cent and in the process many of the local communities were broken up. Reducing the housing stock created a surplus population that could not be accommodated in the inner city, but alternative accommodation had to be found as the shortage of land available within the city boundaries became more acute. The Council began to search elsewhere for possible development land as unlike other major cities there was no New Town for Manchester. Sites beyond Manchester in Lancashire, Cheshire and Derbyshire were investigated and in 1954 the Corporation received letters from each of the County Councils showing both willingness to help and suggesting suitable sites for overspill development in their area.

Between 1953 and 1973 almost 23,500 new dwellings were built by Manchester City Council on 22 overspill sites. The largest of these new communities were at Hattersley (east of Hyde) and Langley to the south of Rochdale.

At Langley, the overspill development aimed to provide 4,000 new homes. By 1963, three blocks of 13-storey flats were added to the scheme pushing the total number of dwellings on the site to 4,700. Similarly, at Hattersley 480 acres of land was subject to a Compulsory Purchase Order and

in 1957 Manchester was given permission to construct 4,150 dwellings.

In the 1970s the voluntary outward movement of population to the suburbs enabled the City Council to move away from its policy of large-scale overspill development. Housing needs were consequently met by building on land within the City boundary.

During this period of housing development the City Council was under considerable pressure from central government to construct as many houses as possible in the shortest period of time. Cost controls imposed by Central Government (the 'Cost Yardstick') also affected the way development was carried out. High densities attracted a higher subsidy for each dwelling constructed. Not surprisingly, given that financial resources were limited, high-rise developments were often seen as the only viable solution.

At the same time pioneering new techniques were introduced using prefabricated concrete panels, constructed in factories and bolted together on site. The aim was to speed up the process of house construction. The national strategy was to employ these methods on a wide scale to meet the post-war housing need and Manchester was no exception. Only in later years were the shortcomings of this approach fully appreciated. For example, it was discovered that the pre-fabricated panels were prone to damage in transit and sometimes failed to bolt together accurately enough to prevent leaking and dampness.

In terms of getting rid of unfit houses the slum clearance programme had been a success. Housing densities had been reduced and open spaces provided.

What had replaced the former congested housing conditions is now often seen as less than ideal. But, it must be remembered that at the time elected members at both central and local government level were keen to promote 'system build' and 'streets in the sky' architecture. Construction companies were keen to sell their factory-produced components as the quickest and most economical way of solving the post-war housing problem. Since their completion, problems of unsuitability of upper floors for disabled people, families with children and the elderly have caused concern and resulted in some developments being badly regarded. The Hulme Crescents are a good example. These have now been demolished in an effort to re-address the problems faced in the Hulme area with entirely different solutions. (See Chapter 9.)

Right: Hattersley overspill estate was built in the late 1950's and early 1960's by Manchester City Council to rehouse people from the slum clearance programme. The picture shows a typical system-built tower block.

Below: Redevelopment of Miles Platting in the 1970's showing the old Victorian houses in the background and newer maisonettes in the foreground.

7 City Centre Redevelopment

In 1961 the Manchester Development Plan was approved by the Ministry of Housing and Local Government with the City Centre section being excluded. More detailed work was required and in 1967 the City Council produced the City Centre Map, a document intended to fill the gap. The major proposals addressed in the 1967 plan related to transport, housing, shopping and commercial activity. Little weight was given to the economic benefits of what remained of the Victorian City. This thinking links closely with the Nicholas Plan and the continued commitment to comprehensive redevelopment in selective areas.

Transport proposals were mainly linked to the development of the road system in and around the centre. A series of major roadways were planned, including a City Centre (Ring) Road to run 20 feet below the line of Portland Street, behind Central Station, through the City Exhibition Hall, over the River Irwell to complete the circle in the City. These road proposals were never implemented mainly owing to the enormous construction costs they would have incurred and the lack of finance available for such projects.

The 1967 City Centre Map highlighted the potential for housing developments in the Regional Centre. It suggested that this would help reverse the trend of suburbanisation, reducing travel to work traffic and bringing life back into the area at all hours. One such scheme built in 1979 by Wimpey created 172 private dwellings on Council-owned land between Byrom Street and Deansgate close to the Granada TV studios.

Manchester's shopping facilities had been badly affected by war damage and the City compared unfavourably with neighbouring towns that had

The Bridgewater Hall, scheduled to open in 1996, will become Manchester's new international concert venue. The project was initiated by Manchester City Council and Central Manchester Development Corporation.

either retained or redeveloped their retail areas. The traditional shopping venue around Market Street was particularly unattractive and congested in the 1960s and in order to deal with these poor conditions, a Comprehensive Development Area was designated by the City Council, so that it could be redeveloped as a whole.

In order to overcome problems of servicing, it was envisaged that a shopping centre, serviced

underground, would be the most appropriate solution. Wilson and Womersley, leading architects of the period, were brought in to design what was to become the largest covered shopping centre in Europe. They designed the Arndale Centre on two levels with a series of malls intersecting in wider squares where exhibitions could be held. The development also comprised a comprehensive indoor market, 200,000 sq. ft of office space, a number of roof-top executive flats and a multi-storey car park. The malls were intended to integrate with existing footways so that traditional lines of pedestrian movement could be maintained.

The major problem with this scheme was that it took nearly 20 years to implement. During this period, surrounding centres were also redeveloped but much more quickly and captured a substantial slice of Manchester's traditional retail trade.

Pedestrianisation was another aspiration of the plan. The problems of traffic congestion were already being felt in the 1960s and it was after seeing pilot schemes in cities such as Amsterdam and Glasgow that Manchester undertook its own experiment. King Street and St Ann's Square were temporarily closed off using concrete pipe sections filled with soil and plants, but it was not until 1976 that a permanent scheme was implemented by the City Council in King Street.

Little progress was made in other areas until the now defunct Greater Manchester Council carried out major surface treatments and environmental improvements to both Market Street in 1983 and St Ann's Square in 1984. Both schemes involved the removal of most vehicles, at least during the working day, and both areas have recently been completely refurbished.

The Arndale Centre, completed in the early 1980's was built as part of the comprehensive redevelopment of the Market Street area. Designed by Wilson and Womersley, it was to become the largest covered shopping centre in Europe.

Following advice given in the Buchanan Report, *Traffic in Towns*, the City Council introduced further measures to alleviate the effects of traffic on the City Centre and tried to separate pedestrians and cars. This was to be achieved by keeping vehicles at ground level and providing pedestrian circulation at a deck level 20 feet higher. Much of the new development constructed at this time incorporated facilities for deck access. A complex pattern of high level entrance and exit to buildings was envisaged with shops and other facilities being incorporated into these corridors. Examples include Piccadilly Plaza, buildings on Mosley Street and the University Precinct. Developments were built with provision of space for future deck access. Some years later when it became apparent that this ideal was too costly to implement, these spaces were filled

The Chinese Arch on Faulkner Street in the heart of Chinatown is one of only three outside China. It cost around £350,000 to construct with contributions from the City Council, Central Government and the Chinese Community.

in and became extensions of the original buildings. Some deck access was constructed and still survives today such as the bridge linking the Arndale Centre to Marks and Spencer.

A popular building style for office developments during the 1950's and early 1960's included a podium at ground and possibly first floor level filling the site boundary and acting as a base for a more slender tower to continue upwards. This type of design reflected government policy on building densities and concern to ensure rights to light. Perhaps the best example of this form of construction is the Piccadilly Plaza complex.

The City Centre Local Plan, published in 1984, provided a framework to help support and regenerate the City Centre following the adverse affects of economic change in the preceding years. This document has guided development in the City Centre up to the present day and formed the basis for the work of the Central Manchester Development Corporation.

An area of the City Centre that was forgotten about and allowed to decline over the years was Castlefield. In 1966 British Rail closed Central Station and in 1975 the Liverpool Road Goods Depot also closed. In 1978, Greater Manchester Council (GMC) bought the Liverpool Road Goods Depot from British Rail and together with the City Council, set about a campaign to promote Castlefield's rich industrial heritage. The City Council designated Castlefield as a Conservation Area in 1979 and the regeneration of the area began. In the same year the City Council resolved to retain and repair the City Exhibition Hall, a Grade II listed building on Liverpool Road and in 1980 proposals were made for the laying out of the Roman Gardens and the reconstruction of the North Gate of the Roman Fort. All these initiatives led to the area being designated as the country's first Urban Heritage Park in 1982.

In 1983 the first phase of the Museum of Science and Industry was completed by the GMC, housed in the restored Liverpool Road Station and former goods depot. The Air and Space Gallery opened soon after within the redeveloped City Exhibition

Hall. Other initiatives that have been undertaken in the area include the Castlefield Hotel, the restoration of canals and tow paths and the development of an Outdoor Events Arena. The Granada company has also invested in Castlefield converting the Grape Street Warehouse into studios, developing the highly popular Granada Studio's Tour built at a cost of over £8 million, and the refurbishing of the Victoria and Albert Warehouse as a hotel. Castlefield has now become one of the major tourist attractions in the North West.

After Central Station was closed the train hall and surrounding grounds became a car park. The building was in a very poor state of repair but the cost of redevelopment was considered to be prohibitive. British Rail sold the site to an Irish racehorse owner and after several further changes of ownership the building and site was eventually acquired by a consortium of the Greater Manchester Council and an insurance company. They promoted a development strategy to bring about the re-use of the Grade II* listed train hall. The new GMex Exhibition and Events Centre opened in 1986 and cost some £20 million. At the time it provided Manchester with England's largest single exhibition hall.

Cultural projects have also played a part in the redevelopment of the City Centre. Chinatown, once a derelict and rundown area, now plays host to one of the largest Chinese communities in the country. With the support of Manchester City Council, the Chinese community has converted former warehouses to restaurants, supermarkets, gift shops, banks, medical and educational facilities and residential accommodation. In 1987, twelve craftsmen from the People's Republic of China constructed the first true Imperial Chinese Arch in Europe. Construction costs amounted to £350,000 with contributions from the City Council, the Department of Environment and the Chinese community.

Manchester's gay and lesbian community are also well catered for in a part of the city commonly referred to as the Gay Village. Restaurants, pubs, night-clubs, cafés and shops are all represented in the areas around Bloom Street and Canal Street.

Recently, Manchester has witnessed a further round of redevelopment in the City Centre which has produced projects such as the Manchester Arena at Victoria and the Bridgewater International Concert Hall.

The Arena is Europe's largest multi-purpose indoor entertainment and sports arena. It was originally conceived in 1989 when Victoria Station was identified as a potential development site for both office development and a small indoor arena. But it was not until 1992, when Manchester was awarded £55 million in support of its Olympic Bid, that the arena concept was developed. Over £35 million of the grant was apportioned to the scheme with a further £35 million being secured from negotiations between central and local government, Bovis North and Vector Investments. The Arena has the capacity to accommodate up to 19,500 spectators and was officially opened on 15 July 1995.

The Bridgewater Hall, Manchester's new international concert hall, is still under construction and will accommodate 2,400 people when it opens in 1996. The project is funded jointly by Manchester City Council and Central Manchester Development Corporation, with a 40 per cent contribution from the European Regional Development Fund. From the foyer of the new development it will be possible to look out of the massive glass frontages onto barges moored in a reconstructed arm of the Rochdale Canal. Rising alongside the hall will be the Great Bridgewater office development which will provide 219,000 sq. ft of office space. These will complete what has been

The CIS Tower on Miller Street was built in 1962 by Sir John Burnet and Tait and Partners with G. S. Hay. At the time it was the tallest office block in Europe.

The Science and Industry Museum in Castlefield was opened in 1983. It won Museum of the Year in 1990 and is currently one of the top tourist attractions in the North West.

known as the Great Bridgewater Initiative, bringing about the regeneration of the Lower Mosley Street area.

The process of redevelopment of the City Centre is a continuous and rapidly changing one. The developments highlighted in this section are only some of the post-war projects which have shaped the way Manchester looks today. What the future hold no-one knows, but if a similar level of development takes place over the next 50 years, the Manchester of tomorrow will be very different from that of today.

8 The Higher Education Precinct

Manchester's Higher Education Precinct is located to the south of the City Centre along Oxford Road and either side of Mancunian Way. There are four principal establishments that make up the precinct – Manchester University, University of Manchester Institute of Science and Technology (UMIST), the Manchester Metropolitan University and the Manchester Royal Infirmary.

After the war the 1945 Plan recognised that there was an urgent need for more university buildings, both educational and residential. Student levels were forecast to rise and there was a severe lack of proper facilities. This recognition continued in the 1961 Plan which identified specific areas to be reserved for the expansion of the Victoria University of Manchester.

In 1967, a development plan was commissioned from Wilson and Womersley by the City Council, Manchester University, UMIST and the United Manchester Hospitals. Their report sought to coordinate new development within the 280 acre site in order to establish a clear identity to the precinct and its surrounding areas. Its fundamental proposal involved the updating of the road system with both Upper Brook Street and Cambridge Street becoming the major routes into the City and Oxford Road becoming the principal service and access route into the Precinct. The plan also proposed to screen off both major routes from the Precinct itself to provide open spaces that would be pleasantly landscaped and free from motor vehicles.

In line with redevelopment proposals for the City Centre, the theme of deck access was also a key

Part of the Education Precinct. Manchester University can be seen in the foreground with the Metropolitan University (left) and UMIST (right) in the middle distance.

feature of the Precinct Plan. Wilson and Womersley believed that pedestrians should be separated from vehicles wherever possible. As a result, buildings were designed to be linked by a series of interconnecting high level walkways which intersected with key points at ground level such as bus stops. It was the architects' vision that students, staff and visitors should be able to walk around the Precinct via high level walkways, through buildings and through landscaped areas set back from the road, without coming into contact with motor vehicles.

The Maths Tower, Computer Centre, Business School and College of Music formed the first part of the integrated upper level walkway system.

In 1974 the plan for the Education Precinct was reviewed by the original consultants and a new document was published setting out proposals for the future. By this time more than £30 million had been invested in the University Precinct with the completion of six science buildings, John Dalton College and the Royal Northern College of Music amongst others. UMIST had transformed the old industrial and residential slums around the Atrincham railway line into a complex of academic, communal and residential buildings grouped around green lawns and paved courts. At the junction of Oxford Road and Booth Street the Precinct Centre was constructed providing shops, offices, library, a public house and many other facilities.

Further improvements were judged to be necessary particularly the provision of new accommodation for students. The original Precinct Plan envisaged 7,000 residents in and around the universities but by 1974 only 2,300 units had been created.

In the early 1980s a further review of the Precinct Plan was undertaken, with the conclusion that a range of complementary activities could be developed alongside higher education uses. A new Science Park, opened in 1984, became the first of these new developments. The aim of this joint public/private venture was to enhance the economic base of the City by utilising the technologies and skills generated in the nearby universities.

The Park currently accommodates 21 small businesses with the potential of doubling this number.

The Higher Education Precinct currently catering for 35,000 students extends over 300 acres with only 10 per cent of the area still available for development. The most recent Action Programme, published in 1994, places a clear emphasis on environmental improvement rather than new building projects. It recommends an investment of £10 million over the next three years in order to enhance the attractiveness of facilities available in this part of the City. Bus priority schemes and new facilities for cyclists are planned as part of an overall scheme to deter cars and through traffic. Landscaping and creative lighting will be used to provide a sense of place and a series of 'gateways' are proposed on routes leading into the precinct.

The Maths Tower on Oxford Street showing the ramp leading to the upper level walkways that linked it to the Computer Centre, Business School, College of Music and University Precinct.

9 Hulme

Hulme grew rapidly in the early nineteenth century to house Manchester's swelling population, as the City's growth was fuelled by the Industrial Revolution. Hulme developed haphazardly as an area of tightly packed terraces and courts, providing cramped and often unsanitary accommodation for migrants coming to the City. Few houses had their own toilets; many had no foundations being laid on bare earth.

Despite this, Victorian Hulme was an important district of the City, close to the major areas of employment with the range of facilities expected in major residential neighbourhoods – shops, churches, pubs and even its own Town Hall. Its high street, Stretford Road, was considered one of Manchester's most important shopping streets.

By the early twentieth century, housing improvement had become a major preoccupation for many local councils in British cities. Subsequently, slum clearance became a new activity for Manchester Corporation in a drive to clear the way for housing renewal.

There had been some new house building in the area by the Council, most notably the Bentley House Estate constructed in the 1940s. However, post-war Britain faced a massive housing crisis and by the early 1960s it was clear that the existing plans for new housing were completely inadequate to meet the national housing shortage. Government Ministers began to apply pressure on local authorities to use the industrialised 'system build' techniques which the building industry was also keenly promoting. These techniques

Opposite: During the 1960's, the redevelopment of Hulme created a 'concrete jungle'. Structural defects and social problems soon became apparent.

Below: Demolition of the notorious Crescents, part of the recent redevelopment of the Hulme area.

The Hulme Crescents surrounded by large areas of open space appeared deceptively attractive when they were built in the mid 1960's. Clearly visible are the high level walkways that allowed transfer between blocks.

used huge factory assembled concrete slabs and panels that slotted together like 'Lego' to construct high rise and deck access blocks up to 20 storeys high. The advantage of system build was its speed.

Councils all over the country, and especially in the inner city areas where land was scarce, embraced this latest fashion as the solution to all their housing problems and embarked on ambitious building programmes that left no time for consultation with residents, many of whom

had already moved out of their homes to over-spill estates. By the early 1960s all remaining terraced houses in Hulme were bulldozed in a clearance programme that left only a few buildings standing.

The vision was for a new Hulme planned around the rigid segregation of vehicles and pedestrians. Tenants were to be housed in flats and maisonettes on interconnecting decks or 'streets in the sky'.

These would be the backbone of social communication where it was assumed that traditional street life would be replicated far above the hazards of traffic. Shopping facilities were to be concentrated around three precincts, Moss Side District Centre and two smaller neighbourhood centres, the traditional shopping areas along Alexandra Road and Princess Road having also succumbed to the bath and chain.

The best known part of the whole development was referred to commonly as the Crescents, four huge curved blocks of flats and maisonettes linked together by walkways and bridges. The architects, Wilson and Womersley, compared their project to Georgian Bath, believing that they had achieved an equivalent solution to satisfy twentieth-century urban living.

By 1972 the redevelopment of Hulme was virtually complete. Over 5,000 new homes had been built in less than eight years and over 3,000 of these were deck access, making Hulme the biggest concentration of this type of housing in the country.

Within months the schemes began to turn into a long nightmare for many of the tenants. The new housing had been hastily constructed using unfamiliar techniques with poor site supervision. Reinforcing bolts and ties that were supposed to hold the panels together were found missing and leaks started to appear. Poor insulation and ventilation caused condensation and huge fuel bills. The development was unsuitable for families, the elderly and the disabled and the 'streets in the sky' never really functioned as envisaged. The poor state of many flats made them hard to let and subsequently the Hulme area suffered considerable decline.

The problems associated with the area grew steadily worse and finally the City Council decided to act through Central Government's 'City Challenge'. This opportunity provided Manchester with the basis of a new start for

The redevelopment of Hulme during the 1960's. In the foreground stand newly built high-rise flats designed to replace older Victorian terraced housing visible in the background.

An example of new housing being provided in Chichester Road by Hulme Regeneration Limited in conjunction with housing associations and private agencies.

up to build 3,000 new homes, new shops, roads, offices and community facilities. The aim is to achieve a close integration of economic and social activities. The new Hulme will offer a wide variety of uses for people to live, shop, work and relax, bringing new income into the local economy. A more traditional pattern of development is being created with streets, squares and buildings of variety and quality that will attract both visitors and residents to the area. New developments will be designed to create a density of people and activity sufficient to sustain the local economy and avoid dead and empty streets and public spaces.

The initiative focuses on an area of about 125 acres which will be cleared and rebuilt in a five year investment programme costing in excess of £200 million with funding from both public and private sources. Nearly three years into its programme, the face of Hulme has already radically altered. Some 1,400 properties have been demolished and 108 acres of land reclaimed. Over 600 homes for rent have been built or are currently under construction and 415 homes have been improved internally.

In addition to the programme of housing renewal, great emphasis is being placed on economic initiatives to sustain the growth of the area. Hulme lies only a short distance from the Higher Education Precinct and the City Centre, and astride the main commuter route to the airport. Key projects include the development of a new high street shopping centre with 100,000 square feet of floorspace and the marketing of a 15 acre site for commercial development. Almost 250 new jobs have already been created.

There is no doubt that the environment of Hulme, both physical and social, is changing rapidly. With the partnership approach being adopted and the involvement of the local community a central element, it is hoped that the problems of the past will not be repeated.

Hulme and subsequent action owes much to the endless campaigning of local residents.

In April 1992 Hulme City Challenge was launched with the help of £37.5 million of Government money. This funding provided a catalyst for a comprehensive programme of initiatives to tackle the various problems of the area through a partnership between the public, private and voluntary sectors and the local community.

Hulme Regeneration Limited was set up by Manchester City Council and AMEC plc as a joint venture to co-ordinate and manage the complex range of initiatives. Ambitious plans were drawn

10 The Greater Manchester Council

The Local Government Bill introduced by a Government White Paper in 1971 prescribed an entirely new system of local government. Under the legislation six new metropolitan counties were set up: West Midlands, Merseyside, West Yorkshire, South Yorkshire, Tyne and Wear and SELNEC (South East Lancashire and North East Cheshire) later to be known as Greater Manchester. On 29 November 1972 the Local Government Bill became an Act of Parliament and the Greater Manchester Metropolitan County was established.

On 12 April 1973 all the members of the first Greater Manchester County Council were elected by the voters in the ten new constituent District Councils; Wigan, Bolton, Bury, Rochdale, Salford, Manchester, Oldham, Trafford, Stockport and Tameside. Finally, on 1 April 1974 the Greater Manchester Council (GMC) came into being; previously there had been around 60 local councils. Its remit covered a wide range of issues, some of which it was solely responsible for and some where it was required to work in conjunction with the districts. The Council was responsible for strategic planning, transportation and major development across the whole of the County. It was responsible for producing the County Structure Plan that set out the key issues affecting the County as a whole and in 1972 a joint working party was set up to undertake the initial preparation work.

Structure Plans were seen by Central Government as a new type of plan which would set down long-term policy objectives, of a general nature, on an area-wide basis. The districts would then work on more specific details in their own 'local' plans.

The first Greater Manchester County Structure Plan was adopted in 1981 with a revision being made in 1986 shortly before the GMC was disbanded. The plan had four main themes. Urban

Central Station in 1968 when it provided both local and national rail links. It was closed by British Rail in 1975 and stood derelict for several years before the site was acquired by the Greater Manchester Council in 1978.

concentration policies aimed to bring development back into urban areas rather than on peripheral open land and backed this up with a strengthening of constraints on greenfield development. Another objective related to the focusing of investment on areas of greatest social deprivation in the central core of the conurbation. The maintenance of the Regional Centre was to be

achieved by the regeneration of the City Centre and adjoining parts of Manchester and Salford in order to provide a more appealing environment to attract people and businesses to the area and thereby stem the decentralisation of activities away from the core. The policies contained in the plan included the removal or re-use of derelict land and obsolescent buildings, the control of air

The new GMex Exhibition and Events Centre opened in the old Central Station building in 1986 and cost some £20 million to redevelop. It provided Manchester with England's largest single exhibition hall.

regeneration in the conurbation. The themes covered by the strategy remain relevant today and have underpinned current planning work at both regional and local levels.

Also in 1981 the GMC produced a document which sought to improve the Medlock Valley. The River Medlock rises in the moorlands of North East Oldham and flows to join the River Irwell in Manchester City Centre. With the rapid expansion of Manchester conurbation during the 1800's and 1900's many areas surrounding the river had suffered extensive despoilation. Therefore, a joint committee led by the GMC, decided that it would undertake a project to clean up the river and its valley in order to provide a major leisure and recreation resource for the City. The aims of the Medlock Valley Plan revolved around increasing the recreational potential and enhancing and conserving the area's natural environment.

A similar initiative was the production of the 1986 Mersey Valley Plan. The Mersey Valley runs for 12 miles through the southern suburbs of Greater Manchester. Again, pressure from urban development had severely affected the use and appearance of open areas and the Mersey Valley Plan aimed to address these problems. Its principal aims were to conserve and enhance the variety of wildlife, to remove dereliction and pollution, and to make the best use of the area for recreational purposes.

In 1974 the GMC inherited an unsatisfactory patchwork quilt of green belt policies across the County and gave high priority to the preparation of a comprehensive new plan, covering the whole County. Work began in 1978 and six years later after the longest public inquiry into a planning issue this area had even seen the Green Belt Plan was finally adopted. The Green Belt was seen as part of the GMC's overall strategy of regeneration, separating built-up areas and halting suburbanisation of the surrounding countryside.

pollution and the cleaning up of river pollution. The final key area that the plan dealt with was related to resource conservation and amenity with proposals to protect open land and reduce energy use.

The Structure Plan was important in setting out a comprehensive strategic framework for

One of the many schemes undertaken by GMC in order to upgrade the environment of the City's waterways and towpaths. A children's playpark was created alongside the Rochdale Canal in Miles Platting.

Though there were occasionally differences of opinion between the City Council and the GMC, much happened during its life which was of benefit to the City. Direct action to reclaim land, plant trees and create footpaths in the Medlock and Mersey Valleys left a legacy of continuing commitment to river valley improvement. Both local plans were eventually incorporated into the 1995 Manchester Plan. The GMC was also a major player in the restoration of Castlefield (see chapter 7) and the redevelopment of GMex. It carried out work to reduce 'blight' caused by years of production of unnecessary road lines, and it followed a policy of encouraging cheap, modern public transport. But its life was brought to an end in 1986 when the Conservative Government abolished the Greater Manchester Council. (See Chapters 7 and 19)

11 Conservation, Listed Buildings and Urban Design

The framework for protecting buildings was established in the Town and County Planning Act, 1947. This legislation was based on the need to identify which buildings of quality remained after the damage sustained during World War II.

Manchester suffered along with many other cities in this respect, but it was the older, better known and obviously dominant buildings which were identified for special listing. Victorian and Edwardian buildings were not well regarded at the time and Manchester, as the most individual Victorian English city, enjoyed only scant recognition for its architectural legacy. The result was a relatively small number of listed buildings – that is buildings of special architectural or historic interest. It took two decades for the appreciation of Victorian and Edwardian architecture to become more widespread. A Department of the Environment survey of the City took place in 1973, with a new list being published in October 1974. The list represented national recognition of the importance of Manchester's buildings and their physical representation of the world's first industrialised city. Approximately 600 buildings were included in the list.

A survey of the city in the early 1990s by the Department of National Heritage resulted in a total of 960 buildings being listed in 1994, nearly 50 per cent of which are in the City Centre. Even

Royal Mill, a grade 2 listed building on Redhill Street. This former cotton mill was built in 1912 on the banks of the Rochdale Canal in Ancoats.

Refuge Assurance Building, Oxford Street, Grade 2*. Insurance company offices built in 1891 and designed by Alfred Waterhouse.

though the numbers game is not relevant in respect of listed buildings, the new list more accurately reflects the undoubted architectural qualities of buildings which line the City's streets.

In a departure from previous practice, the Department of National Heritage recently canvassed the public's opinion on the listing of post-war buildings nationally. Four buildings designed in the 1950s and 1960s are on the proposed list in Manchester and others may yet be added. Three are office buildings, including the CIS tower on Miller Street. The other is Oxford Road Railway Station.

The architectural form and the historical association of individual buildings in the City are significant in establishing its character, but the relationship of the buildings to each other and to the streets and spaces around which they are located, determine the physical form of the City.

This appreciation of the wider character of areas, as opposed to individual buildings, was formally recognised in the Civic Amenities Act of 1967 when local planning authorities were permitted to designate 'Conservation Areas' – areas of special architectural or historic interest, the character or appearance of which it is desirable to preserve or enhance. In the early national documentation about Conservation Areas, reference was made to whole town centres, squares, terraces and smaller groups of buildings, often centred on listed buildings, pleasant groups of other buildings, open spaces, trees, an historic street pattern, a village or features of archaeological interest as examples which contribute to the special character of an area.

The genteel chocolate-box areas in some authorities were not part of Manchester's character so it was with some caution that the City designated its first Conservation Areas in 1970. St Ann's Square and Chorlton Green had this honour, closely followed by St John Street, Upper King Street and Didsbury St James. Further areas were designated in the early 1970s, followed by a period of consolidation until the 1980s, since when a steady increase in the number of designations has

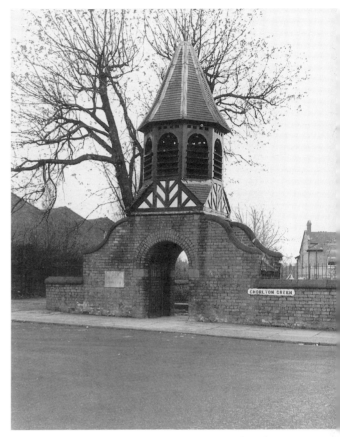

Gate House and Bell Turret at Chorlton Green listed as Grade 2. Part of the former Chuch of St. Clement built in 1779 and demolished in 1949.

reflected the growing appreciation and understanding of the role that Manchester played in the development of Western industrial and commercial life during the Industrial Revolution and in the nineteenth century.

At the present time the City has designated 29 Conservation Areas, 14 of which are in the City Centre, many of the areas achieving their status as a consequence of the cotton industry which so dominated all aspects of the City's life in the nineteenth century. Many have been the subject of environmental improvement which has added to the character of the area. Most notable has been the Castlefield area, which in the first ten years after its designation in 1979 had over £30 million of enhancement. Much more has been spent since.

Above: No 378 Deansgate a Grade 2 listed building. Former Congregational Chapel built in 1858 on the River Medlock, in Castlefield. Now renovated into a recording studio.

Below: The Towers (Shirley Institute), Wilmslow Road, Didsbury, Grade 2. The Mansion built between 1868 and 1872 by Thomas Worthington now provides elegant office accommodation.

First Church of Christ Scientist, Daisy Bank Road, Rusholme, Grade 1. Built in 1903, the premises are now a cultural centre.

Some of the more recent designations highlight the industrial archaeology of the City – a major attraction to visitors from abroad. It is likely that further designations will continue to reflect this aspect of the City's heritage. Indeed the concept is strengthened by the Department of National Heritage's recent building survey which greatly increased the number of listed archaeology artefacts.

The noted historian, Asa Briggs, stated in his book *Victorian Cities* that 'The Industrial Cities of Britain were by no means all alike. Manchester was the shock city of the Industrial Revolution, but it was not typical. Its real interest lies in its individuality.' That individuality developed as a consequence of the cotton industry, the dominance of which was so clear that the larger area was referred to as 'Cottonopolis'. The industry was allowed to prosper as much by the location of the City as by the industry and inventive genius of its workforce.

Medieval Manchester is poorly represented in terms of buildings but the curving road pattern remains in the area centred on the Cathedral which contrasts with the Georgian and Victorian street grid pattern which dominates the rest of the City Centre. The grid has an overlying fan shape which converges around the GMex site and the southern end of the City Centre.

Much of Georgian Manchester was demolished by the Victorians at a time when the City was expanding at an unprecedented rate in the late eighteenth and nineteenth centuries. They lined the streets with buildings, so that the 'street wall' became complete and this, rather than individual buildings, really established the City's physical character. That character remains to this day.

Victorian buildings were designed in either the classical or gothic style. The Free Trade Hall is an example of the former and the Town Hall the latter.

Much of this character and feel for the City appeared to have been lost in buildings which were erected in the 1950s to the 1970s, but more recent developments in Quay Street, Peter Street, Fountain Street and Deansgate have tried to re-establish those qualities which made Victorian streets so successful, but they have done so in a manner which is thoroughly modern and which does not copy past styles.

Also in recent years many of the Victorian warehouse buildings have been modified for new uses. No longer suitable for the purpose for which they were originally designed, they have been adapted for residential, hotel and entertainment uses whilst still retaining much of their character.

Just as old buildings are being recognised as helping to create the City's character by being put to new uses, so other industrial artefacts like the canals and mills are now understood to possess economic benefits for the City in the next century.

Left: Clayton Hall, Ashton New Road, Clayton, Grade 2*. The original manor house was probably built in the 1400's. Restored during the 19th and 20th Centuries, it now provides two dwellings.

Below: No 190 Cheetham Hill Road, Manchester Jewish Museum, Grade 2. Built in 1889 this Spanish and Portuguese Synagogue currently houses the Manchester Jewish Museum.

With the construction of the country's first 'cut' canal in 1760, the Bridgewater brought a new life to the Castlefield area. Even though this area fell into decline in the twentieth century, recognition of the historical importance of the canals, railways and other industrial artefacts led to its designation as a Conservation Area in 1979 and its regeneration since then has been cited as an incentive to other parts of the City and to other towns both in Britain and abroad.

Industrial areas such as Ancoats, where cotton mills, canals and residential accommodation were all located from 1800 onwards and which have declined since the 1920s, can take encouragement from the economic regeneration of Castlefield. The restoration of characterful areas like these provide a powerful tourist magnet, with the economic benefits that the influx of visitors can bring.

12 Derelict Land and East Manchester

East Manchester is one of the key areas in the City where there are opportunities for major change, regeneration and improvement. The area covers over $6\frac{1}{2}$ square miles to the east of the City Centre and includes the wards of Beswick and Clayton, Bradford, Gorton North, Newton Heath and Miles Platting.

East Manchester reached its zenith at the end of the nineteenth century when it was one of Britain's main centres of heavy engineering, power, transport and chemical industries. From the middle of the twentieth century, the decline in the traditional industries hit hard with over 24,000 jobs being lost between 1974 and 1984. At the same time, clearance of large areas of Victorian terraced housing made way for new council housing estates such as Miles Platting, redeveloped in the 1950s, and Beswick in the 1970s.

In the early 1980s, problems stemming from unemployment, derelict land and lack of investment were addressed through the East Manchester Initiative, a partnership between the Council and Central Government which sought to target Urban Programme grants to the area. This work was co-ordinated under the East Manchester Planning Framework. This highlighted the major problems that the area was facing at the time and went on to detail the objectives which the Council would follow in order to upgrade it.

Some of the environmental improvements undertaken in the East Manchester Area during recent years.

The basic objectives of the plan were fourfold: to assist in the economic recovery of the area; to improve the environment; to improve access and mobility; and to enhance the housing stock. These objectives revolved around the reclamation of derelict land, left vacant by the declining industrial base. It also involved the continued reclamation of the areas around both the Medlock Valley and the Rochdale Canal near Miles Platting in order to enhance their roles as recreational resources.

The housing strategy that was adopted in the plan was based on the improvement of certain areas of existing housing stock, along with the designation of land for further housing develop-

Above: Built in the 1960's Fort Ardwick provided over 600 deck access properties in a single block but experienced similar structural and social problems to the Hulme Crescents. They are pictured here shortly before demolition.

Left: The new National Cycling Centre in Eastlands built to support the Manchester Olympic Games bids and helping to regenerate East Manchester.

In 1992, East Manchester was chosen as the prime location for the major sports and social facilities associated with the 2000 Olympic Games Bid. The East Manchester Regeneration Strategy was also published in the same year and this detailed an innovative programme of sports-led regeneration to ensure that hosting the world's premier sports event would lead to major sustained improvement for the local area. The overall objectives remained similar to those put forward in 1983 with the main ones being:

- Stimulating economic and business development.

- Securing effective land use, environmental and infrastructural improvements.

- Encouraging diversity in housing provision and social conditions.

- Developing skilled and self-reliant communities.

The aim of the whole regeneration strategy was to provide for up to 3.5 million square feet of new industrial and commercial floorspace offering up to 10,000 new jobs and 2,000 new houses. This

ment, including the encouragement of private sector involvement for the first time in many decades. Areas in Miles Platting, Beswick and Clayton, and Openshaw were released for new development and over the period between 1982 and 1991 over £48 million had been spent on refurbishing the 1950s housing estates in the Miles Platting area alone.

was to be achieved by encouraging inward investment to the area through the development of a marketing strategy for East Manchester and a move towards the establishment of a medical science and technology park. There was also a proposal to focus regeneration on a number of specific areas. For example a new development including housing, retail and leisure uses would be targeted at the Miles Platting area and the Ancoats redevelopment would be led by the refurbishment of redundant mill and warehouse buildings. This initiative has gained pace in the last two years with a successful bid for Single Regeneration Budget status for the whole of Ancoats and Miles Platting in partnership with local community groups and private sector interests.

In terms of housing proposals the plan set out a number of key issues that needed to be addressed. Development sites have been ident-ified throughout the area for a wide range of new housing and facilities for residents as well as undertaking improvement works to the older housing stock in areas such as Openshaw, Colly-hurst and Newton Heath.

Despite the ultimate decision to take the 2000 games to Sydney, East Manchester has gained enormous benefits from the bid and key elements of the Regeneration Strategy are now becoming reality:

- Over £40 million of Special Government Grant to acquire and clear the main 150 acre Eastlands site and to construct the new National Cycling Centre at the Velodrome.

- Completion of the Intermediate Ring Road, a new dual carriageway linking East Manchester to the national motorway network.

- Promotion of a new National Stadium to be funded through the lottery and allied to the City's successful bid to host the 2002 Commonwealth Games.

- Proposed East Manchester Metrolink line promoted by the Passenger Transport Authority.

- Completion of major derelict land reclamation schemes such as Ardwick West and East Goods Yards, now being developed for new industrial uses.

13 Olympic and Commonwealth Games Bids

One of the more unusual, though significant influences on the planning process in Manchester in the late 1980's and 1990's has been the City's two bids to host the Olympic Games for the years 1996 and 2000 and its recently successful bid for the 2002 Commonwealth Games. This chapter sets out the background to Manchester's various bids and the contribution of the bids to the regeneration of the City.

The 1996 Olympic Games Bid

The 1996 Bid was initiated by a group of private sector companies largely, at least in the early stages, without involvement from the City Council. The Bid was seen as an ideal opportunity to promote Manchester on a world stage to the benefit of the City, the private sector and ultimately those living and working in the City. The venue strategy presented in the bid documentation submitted to the International Olympic Committee in February 1990, providing for the main stadium, arena and swimming pool to be located outside the City's boundaries on a site known as Dumplington (with other facilities being dispersed around the region at Liverpool, Chester, Wigan and North Wales), seemingly flew in the face of the Olympic ideal which favoured the compact venue with facilities in easy travelling distance of each other and the athletes' village.

The City Council became involved with the then Bid Committee at about the time the Bid Document was being finalised and worked with other local authorities on an implementation strategy for the venue plan in the months leading up to the IOC decision in September 1990. As history records, the IOC awarded the 1996 Games to Atlanta, and although Manchester's bid received very little support, including only limited support from the Government, the experience of bidding

was considered to have been extremely positive in terms of Manchester's profile although less than effective in terms of creating any real legacy for the City. It was also useful in generating support for the idea of the Olympic Bid locally, which was essential if this process was to be repeated.

The 2000 Olympic Games Bid

In late 1990, the City Council with the full backing of former members of the Bid Committee and the private sector announced its intention to bid for the 2000 Olympics. It committed itself at the same time to the delivery of three major facilities which would lend credibility to its bid as well as ensure that there would be a real legacy for Manchester from the bidding process irrespective of whether or not the bid was successful.

Working directly with a newly formed Bid Committee, the City Council led the process of review of the 1996 venue strategy in the light of feedback from the 1996 bid. This involved an audit of sports facilities throughout Greater Manchester and the region and resulted in a radical re-shaping of the venue strategy with the primary focus being the development of the main Olympic facilities on an inner city regeneration site at Eastlands in East Manchester. The intention was that this would be the location of the main stadium, velodrome and other ancillary facilities with the athletes' village being located in an area fondly described as 'the dog bone' either side of the Ashton Canal between Eastlands and the City Centre in a mix of refurbished warehouses and new developments. The intention was that the implementation of such a strategy, as well as being a basis for a successful bid, would be a powerful tool of inner city regeneration. The eventual venue strategy was developed after Manchester defeated London to become the British candidate city in the spring of 1991. It envisaged 21 of the 25 required venues being located within an 'Olympic Ring' which had the City Centre at its heart. A total of 15 sports were to be held in or adjacent to the City Centre. The venue strategy was drawn up to meet three primary considerations: compactness; caring for the environment; legacy and after-use.

An artists impression of the proposed Millennium Stadium in Eastlands. Designed to hold 65,000 people it was intended to form a centrepiece for the Olympic Games.

Firstly, feedback from the 1996 bidding process suggested that the ideal Olympic venue strategy was one where the majority of facilities were located within easy travelling distance of the athletes' village and of each other. With 21 of the 25 venues being located within the Olympic Ring, Manchester's strategy represented a very attractive proposition for the IOC. The aim was to ensure that athletes and spectators spent their time at the sports – not travelling between them. Secondly, environmental issues were a key concern in the preparation of a venue strategy. The majority of venues were connected by public transport and the environmental impact of all facilities was assessed. The intention was that the venue strategy would have the minimum impact on the environment both through the location of venues and the use of inner city sites requiring regeneration. In addition, an Environmental Charter was drawn up which set out the principles on which the venue strategy would be implemented in the event of Manchester's bid being successful.

Thirdly, Manchester's venue strategy involved the use of new and existing venues. Each facility had an assured after-use which was not necessarily sports or leisure related. In other words, the requirement for 25 venues was exploited to the maximum to deliver uses which Manchester needed in any event irrespective of whether it hosted the Games. Thus the legacy of the Games

to Manchester was to be new and enhanced sports facilities, regional infrastructure improvements, student accommodation, social and private sector housing and extended museum and exhibition space.

Manchester's bid was technically very sound and was highly commended by the IOC's Evaluation Commission.

The previous chapter describes the City Council's approach to the development of the Eastlands site, and in particular, the international development competition which resulted in the appointment of a world class development team. Proposals for the Eastlands site involved its development as a major sports/leisure park with the Stadium at its heart. The principles of this development are now reflected in Manchester's Unitary Development Plan.

The strategy for the redevelopment of Eastlands showing the proposed Millennium Stadium (centre), the velodrome (right) and Bradford Gasworks (top).

Manchester received strong support from the Government both in terms of lobbying from the Prime Minister and senior members of the Cabinet and, more importantly for Manchester, £70 million of additional resources which enabled the construction of the National Cycling Centre, Europe's largest indoor arena at Victoria Station and the acquisition, clearance and preparation of the site at Eastlands required for the Stadium. The process of building the City's international profile, which the first Olympic Bid had started, was also taken a great deal further by the second Bid. Although Manchester's bid was unsuccessful, these two facilities and the progress made in preparing for the Stadium were the real legacies for the City.

The 2002 Commonwealth Games Bid

Within a month of the award of the 2000 Olympics, Manchester was invited by the Commonwealth Games Council for England to bid to become the English candidate city for the 2002 Commonwealth Games. Although a smaller event than the Olympic Games, the City Council decided that similar benefits could be secured for Manchester, particularly in terms of the development of the Eastlands site, and it therefore decided to submit a bid. On 2 February 1994, Manchester once more defeated London and became the English candidate city for the 2002 Games.

The venue strategy was refined to provide for the majority of venues being located in, or adjacent to, the City Centre with the Eastlands site remaining the focus of major facilities for the Games. The athletes' village proposal was also modified to reflect the smaller number of competitors but the intention set out in the bid documentation is that the village will be in a similar location as was proposed for the Olympics but in a smaller area at the City Centre end of the 'dog bone'.

Manchester's bid gained momentum within the first few months of the campaign and, following a very positive technical evaluation by the Commonwealth Games Federation, the City was awarded the 2002 Commonwealth Games on 3 November 1995.

14 Area Regeneration

Many of Manchester's inner city areas have been redeveloped since the end of World War II. Hulme and East Manchester are covered elsewhere in the book (see chapters 9 and 12). This chapter focuses on other parts of the inner city where renewal has been ongoing.

Ardwick and Longsight

To tackle the enormous post-war housing problem it was clear by the early 1960s that an ambitious programme of clearance was needed. Initially, areas forming a semicircle around the City Centre were chosen for renewal, and while often more is known about Hulme, change in Ardwick was equally comprehensive.

The old Victorian terraced housing was swept away to be replaced by the huge 'yellow' brick Council estates that we can see today. In other locations, high-rise developments such as Fort Ardwick were erected. Fort Ardwick provided over 600 properties in a single deck-access block, but soon developed all the problems associated with system building. Eventually, the Council viewed demolition as the only solution.

In recent years more traditional low-rise developments built by housing associations have replaced Fort Ardwick Estate. Modernisation has taken place at New Bank Street and Chorlton-on-Medlock under the Estate Action Programme. Convoluted and confusing layouts are responsible for many of the problems currently experienced. The

Flats on Palgrave Avenue in Monsall before stuctural alterations.

new approach is to remove pedestrian walkways, unsightly open spaces and unused areas in order to achieve housing which fronts onto busier streets providing natural surveillance. The objective of planning in the 1990s is the creation of successful neighbourhoods where people want to live.

Moss Side

Within a distance of two miles as you move west to east across Moss Side there are examples of most types of housing solutions that we have seen in Britain since World War II. The tower

The Palgrave Avenue flats after they have been decapped and significantly upgraded.

Alexandra Park Estate, although the layout fashions for estates that were prevalent at the time are now being reassessed to improve them. The shift in emphasis towards renewal of older housing, begun in the late 1970s, is clearly evident in the Victorian streets off Princess Road. Elsewhere, there are pockets of small scale redevelopment chiefly undertaken by housing associations during the last 10–15 years.

Redevelopment in Moss Side provided a pattern of land use based on segregation of pedestrians and vehicles with a hierarchy of roads, shopping and other facilities. Today the Council prefers to take a more sensitive approach to renewal. Local area regeneration now combines housing renewal and radical redesign within a broader strategy addressing core problems such as unemployment, poverty, crime and negative images of the area as well as improvement of social facilities. Hopefully this will create a sustainable, balanced and self-reliant neighbourhood which can be integrated within and contribute fully to the prosperity of the City.

North Manchester Initiative

Another major area renewal project that is currently being undertaken through Government funding is the North Manchester Regeneration Initiative. This scheme represents the largest sector of land available for development in the City covering an area of more than three square miles. It comprises the neighbourhoods of Monsall, Harpurhey, Lightbowne and Charlestown within which over 170 acres of development land are available.

The area has a population of 20,000 and it currently experiences a number of problems including high unemployment, a low level of owner-occupation and poor housing choice. The Council has judged that there is a need for major regeneration in order to increase housing choice and stem the loss of population experienced in recent years.

blocks on the edge of the area give way to sites formerly occupied by deck-access properties alongside Moss Side District Centre built in the 1960s. In the following decade there was a reaction to system building with the construction of low-rise, low-density municipal housing on the

The Single Regeneration Budget (SRB) bid for North Manchester, which has generated the main public funding for this project, was put forward as a partnership between many players including Manchester City Council, Bellway Urban Renewal and East Manchester Partnership. Available land will be utilised for new private and social housing as well as a range of employment generating industrial and commercial uses. All schemes will be developed in line with the new City Development Guide (see chapter 22). The SRB bid for £30 million will underpin private-sector led regeneration and is expected to create up to 2,500 new houses and associated improvements that are intended to transform the character and image of the area.

The strategy will generate higher quality private-sector housing predominantly for sale but with some aimed at the rented sector. A better mix of housing tenure will also be promoted along with higher housing densities in order to create sustainable commercial and social facilities, support for existing local services and new neighbourhoods. New roads are proposed in order to open up sites for development by improving access into the area.

Cheetham

The latest SRB Bid relates to the areas of Cheetham and Broughton. Manchester City Council and Salford City Council have worked in partnership and drawn up a joint scheme for an area which straddles the boundary between the two authorities. It was submitted to the Department of the Environment in 1995 and is currently being appraised. A decision on funding is expected shortly.

15 Environmental Improvements

The quality of the environment is a crucial factor in attracting new activities to an area and to its future economic and commercial well-being. Manchester City Council's approach to environmental improvements is based on two perspectives. The first is concerned with improving the local environment for the benefit of people who live, work or visit the City. The second involves the contribution that action in Manchester can make to the solution of global environmental problems. The two are often connected; for example, the treatment of derelict land brings it back into use, saves loss of green land through development and removes eyesores from the local environment.

To achieve this end, many projects have already been implemented and others are currently proposed. This section concentrates on a number of improvements that have taken place in the City Centre in recent years including Albert Square, Market Street and St Ann's Square. It also details some of the smaller scale initiatives undertaken.

Albert Square

In 1984 the City Council decided to undertake a refurbishment of the Albert Square area. The Square contains a mixture of nineteenth-century French Renaissance and Venetian Gothic architecture. It has as its centrepiece the Albert Memorial, flanked by statues of James Fraser (former Bishop of Manchester), John Bright (Quaker Statesman), Oliver Heywood (Benefactor) and W. E. Gladstone (Liberal Prime Minister), but it is dominated

Albert Square in 1985 when traffic circulated around the central square and parking was allowed in front of the Town Hall.

Albert Square in 1987 after repaving work with traffic directed around the outside
of the Square.

by one of the world's finest Town Halls on its east side.

The problems that the area faced at that time were traffic congestion and parking, poor surface material conditions and an unsuitable overall appearance for the setting of fine buildings. The City Council saw Albert Square as a venue for public gatherings including theatrical and musical performances, fairs and various street entertainment and to this end set about designing a space suitable for these types of activity.

The proposals abolished all traffic and parking from the area in front of the Town Hall and diverted it around the other three edges of the Square making the pedestrian area as large as possible. This was repaved using a combination of granite setts and natural stone paving flags. Extra trees sponsored by the Manchester Evening News were planted to soften and structure the central open space and seating was provided on all four sides of the Square.

Market Street

After many years of debate much of the traffic movement in Market Street was removed in 1981 and the surface was repaved in 1983 by the former Greater Manchester Council. Before it was refurbished in 1993, the street surfaces were badly worn; it was cluttered with an unco-ordinated mixture of traders, telephone kiosks, seats and trees and it was congested with high numbers of pedestrians and vehicles supposedly banned from the area between 10.00 am and 4.00 pm but not enforced. As a consequence it was decided to implement a major environmental improvement scheme along the street and to hold a limited design competition. The winning scheme included the following design principles:

- The creation of clearly defined, safe unobstructed routes for pedestrians which were to be surfaced in a combination of red and blue brick and concrete paviours.

- The creation of a clearly defined vehicular route on the Arndale side of the

street for emergency vehicles, and on the other side for service vehicles.

- The improvement and co-ordination of existing street furniture resited in such a way that it improved the environment of the area.

- The creation of three 'squares' to form circulation areas and focal points.

Kerb upstands were eliminated to allow easy access for all people along the street. The overall cost of the scheme was met by a number of organisations with major contributions from P&O Shopping Centres and Manchester City Council.

St Ann's Square

St Ann's Square is Georgian in origin but lies in the heart of the Victorian City Centre. The presence of St Ann's Church, banks and the Royal Exchange Theatre creates a varied and active atmosphere.

There have been aspirations to improve the Square since the 1950s and several attempts had been made in the 1960s and 1970s to restrict the numbers of vehicles entering the space and to improve the environment by planting trees and introducing better quality paving. Much of this was of a temporary nature. It was not until 1984 that a comprehensive scheme was put in place to repave, plant trees and install appropriate street furniture, the work being carried out by the former Greater Manchester Council. This scheme was successful in the early years, but with continued vehicle abuse in the Square the area needed repair on a regular basis. In 1993, with the agreement of the owners of the buildings surrounding the Square, the City Council decided to carry out a full refurbishment of the space and of the surrounding streets and to pedestrianise the

Above left: Market Street in 1993 with badly worn pavement surfaces and poor quality seating.

Left: Market Street after refurbishment in 1993 with new pavement surfaces, coordinated street furniture and an obelisk as a centrepiece.

main body of the Square. Traffic Regulation Orders were revised to restrict servicing use of Exchange Street to the hours of 7.00 am to 11.00 am and create a traffic-free environment for most of the day.

In order to pedestrianise the Square it was necessary to create a turning circle for vehicles entering Exchange Street and the Boer War Memorial statue became the obvious centre point of that circle. The curved form was repeated at the church end of the Square and pushed out into St Ann Street so that a closer relationship could be established between the church and the Square. It was also considered important to recreate the pavements even though these were to be flush with the other surfaces of the Square. In order to protect the statue at the centre of the turning circle it was felt necessary to install visually strong protective elements in the form of stone spheres. All other items of street furniture – benches, planters and bases to bins – were also made of buff coloured stone so as to fit in with the surrounding building colours.

The cost of the works to date has been almost £1 million which excludes the cost of a new water feature to be located in the centre of the Square. A significant financial contribution was forthcoming from building owners notably MEPC and Prudential Insurance and users surrounding the Square. The scheme's success was underlined recently when it won the Pedestrianisation category of the 1995 National Street Design Awards.

Community Based Work

The City Council has encouraged the involvement of the community in small-scale environmental improvements. In 1986 they produced a Community Landscapes Pack which was updated in 1990. This Pack, along with the City Council funded Community Initiatives Fund, Annual Tree Plant and Schools Challenge (see chapters 16 and 21) are just some of the initiatives launched through this scheme. Projects undertaken to date are varied and diverse ranging from the improvement and opening up of woodland in a built-up area of Wythenshawe to the development of a nature study area in Chapel Street Primary School grounds in Levenshulme.

St Ann's Square as it was in 1990 with poor quality surfaces and a lack of seating.

The City Council has set out its priorities for future environmental improvements in the 1995 Manchester Plan. These aims include amongst others:

- The creation of a network of recreational open spaces.

- The promotion of measures which will lead to a safer environment for all who live in and use the City.

- The promotion of improvements aimed at providing better conditions for disabled people.

- The further enhancement of the environment of the City Centre with an emphasis on improving conditions for pedestrians.

The schemes highlighted in this chapter are only a small sample of the environmental improvements which have taken place over the last 50 years. Other major initiatives include improvements to the river valleys of the Irk, Medlock, Mersey and Bollin as well as action to reclaim other waterways such as the canal system in Castlefield. These projects are referred to elsewhere in this book.

Opposite: View of St Ann's Square as it is now with coordinated street furniture, and improved pavements. The design achieved an award in the Pedestrianisation category of the 1995 National Street Design competition.

16 Community Involvement and Access for Disabled People

Over the past 15 years community involvement has been an important part of the planning process and one that Manchester City Council has been keen to promote. Many initiatives from the day to day control of development and production of the 1995 Manchester Plan to schemes such as the annual Tree Plant are intended to involve the public and keep them well informed.

In terms of information, over the years the Council has produced many leaflets and documents to advise the public on what is happening and how they can be involved. For example, during the late 1980's and early 1990's the Council's development initiatives in East Manchester were documented in a quarterly publication called *East Manchester News*. This ran for a total of seven issues and included sections on what was happening locally, recollections from local residents and, in a light-hearted vein, the (H)Adventures of Billy Bradshaw. The *City Planning News* was another information newspaper published to promote the Manchester Plan during the stages when it was being put together, and to invite comments from the general public, action groups and commercial interests.

A range of new initiatives were introduced by the Council in 1985 to encourage direct involvement of the public in the process of environmental improvement. They were financed through the Government's Urban Programme. In May of that year the Community Initiatives Fund (CIF) was launched, providing grants up to £25,000 for schools, local groups and other organisations

Below: The Council's annual Tree Plant events were designed to raise awareness and encourage the planting of a large number of trees

Right: Local residents are consulted over the redevelopment of Hulme.

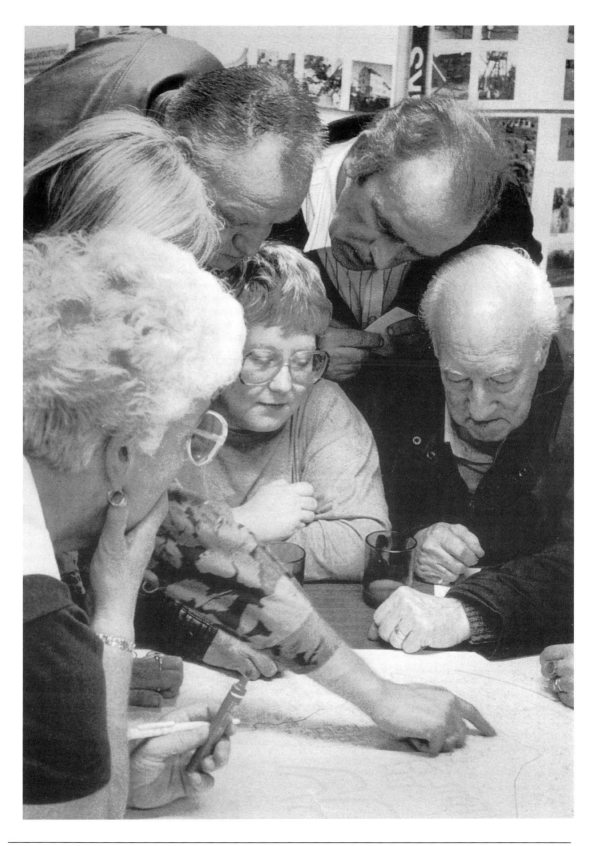

wishing to carry out their own schemes. A Community Landscapes Information Pack was published at the same time to promote the initiative and guide implementation.

In an effort to raise awareness of environmental issues to an even wider audience, the Council allocated a small sum of money to promote a community Tree Plant event. Young trees were provided by the Council free of charge. Schools, local community groups and businesses were invited to suggest appropriate sites and provide volunteers to undertake the planting. The initiative proved a great success and Tree Plant became an annual event in the Council's calendar of environmental action. Projects ranged in size from a small number of standard trees to large numbers of whips planted en masse to create new woodland.

In 1992 the Council published a major document entitled 'Taking Involvement Seriously' which was widely circulated amongst Council Officers. It included examples of good practice from many areas of Council activity and set out guidelines for those seeking to work with the public. It also made a clear distinction between the provision of information and the processes of consultation and participation. These principles have been incorporated into many of the planning initiatives undertaken in recent years. Production of the 1995 Manchester Plan is a good example. Here, the Council embarked on a massive consultation process to involve as many interests as possible. Similarly, the development control process aims to inform as many local people as possible about development proposals which are likely to affect themselves and their neighbourhood. This approach is carried through to the Planning Committee stage where members of the public have the right to speak to local councillors on matters of concern.

Improving Access for Disabled People

During the 1980s the Council pursued a broad policy of equal opportunities both in terms of recruitment and the delivery of services. This included a range of initiatives designed to improve access facilities for disabled people. Disabled Access Grants (DAG) were made available

to community groups and local businesses in order to carry out appropriate enhancements such as ramps, wider doors and suitable toilet facilities. This process will continue, albeit on a more selective basis, because the resources available for this programme have been reduced.

The development control process also has a major role to play in ensuring that new development schemes take the access needs of disabled people seriously. Plans are carefully scrutinised from this perspective and in some cases consultations take place with representatives of disabled people's interests. The Planning Department itself has employed an Access Officer to help and advise with this work. If submitted schemes are inadequate in these terms negotiation takes place with developers to improve them. To this end a design guide has been published and widely distributed.

The Council itself has set examples of good practice by opening up the Town Hall to all members of the community and making a major investment in new footways and dropped curbs. All new public buildings are designed to ensure unrestricted access for disabled people and the Council continues to work closely with community representatives to take proper account of everybody's needs.

Whilst there have been debates for a long time about what community involvement in planning means and about how best to achieve it, the case for seeing this as an essential part of the process no longer needs to be made. It is worth remembering, however, that this was not the case during the redevelopment period in the inner city, which carried on into the 1970s. Not only is some of this now established in planning law, but we now know that local knowledge and understanding is a very valuable part of the planning process and can be a major contributor to it. In addition the Council now accepts that a consultative approach to planning decision-making is one of the rights that people have as citizens of Manchester.

Opposite: Aerial Manchester An aerial view of the City Centre with the Midland Hotel and the Town Hall complex visible in the foreground. In the distance the white roof of the Nynex Arena and flats above the Arndale Centre can be seen clearly.

Left: Manchester Metropolitan University Library, Chorlton Street: Architect–G. Mills 1993.

Below left: Offices, 49 Peter Street: Architect–G. Mills 1992.

Below: Airport Railway Station, Ringway: Architect–ASL 1993.

Offices and Shops, 41–43 King Street: Architects–Buttress, Fuller, Alsop 1994.

15 Quay Street: Architect–Stephenson Architecture 1992.

Nynex Arena   Opened in July 1995 the Manchester Nynex Arena is Europe's largest multi-purpose indoor entertainment and sports venue.

Interior of Trinity Court   John Dalton Street: Architect–Stephenson Architecture 1993.

18 Central Manchester Development Corporation

Britain's urban development corporations were created in the 1980's to tackle urban decline in major cities, where blight and dereliction often occurred alongside prosperous areas which attracted substantial levels of private investment. Their brief was to act as catalysts for the regeneration of these run-down areas, using public funds to improve environments and, working with private sector developers, to bring disused land and buildings back into productive use.

In June 1988 Central Manchester Development Corporation (CMDC) was set up by Central Government to regenerate nearly 500 acres of land and buildings in the southern sector of the City Centre stretching in an arc from Piccadilly Station to Pomona Docks and including six Conservation Areas with over 90 listed buildings and structures. The decaying warehouses, offices, mills and railway viaducts were set against a canvas of contaminated land, neglected waterways and other problems typical of this kind of area.

At the same time, the area also had its assets. Its buildings and spaces included elements of potentially very good environmental quality which were capable of being used to promote refurbishment schemes for a range of activities. These uses included housing, in which some interest was already being shown, and which was undoubtedly helped by the proximity of parts of the CMDC area to the City's three main universities. And in Castlefield, the area contained Britain's first Urban Heritage Park, where considerable public and private money had already been spent on major attractions such as the Museum of Science and Industry and Granada Studio Tours, but where much still needed to be done to maintain and build on this momentum.

In setting about its task, the Corporation first engaged in widespread consultation in formulating a Development Strategy which complemented the City Council's 1984 City Centre Local Plan.

In addition to its planning powers, CMDC has had a range of other powers which work in combination to achieve regeneration. Critical amongst these have been its grant giving powers and its powers of direct expenditure on environmental improvements. Its grant giving powers have played a major role in encouraging housing uses back into this part of the City Centre, to the point at which this may well have become self-sustaining. Its environmental improvement

Left: The Eastgate Building in Castlefield before refurbishment.

Right: The Eastgate Building after transformation into studio offices.

The site on the banks of the Ashton Canal where Piccadilly Village now stands.

powers have seen major changes take place, for example in the Castlefield area and along the banks of the Rochdale Canal.

Proof of the effectiveness of CMDC's work and its success in injecting extra resources into Manchester are very evident. The Bridgewater Concert Hall and adjacent Great Bridgewater office development – secured in partnership with the City Council and totalling £100 million of investment – lie at the heart of a major extension to the City's central business district. Successful residential developments have brought thousands of people back to live in the City Centre. Historic canals, rivers and their surroundings have been rescued from decay and disuse. Castlefield has emerged as the setting for successful housing and office developments and now attracts over two

million leisure visitors a year. Schemes large and small have improved pedestrian access and calmed traffic. In the eight years of its operation, over £420 million of investment has come to Manchester in the CMDC area.

One of the many projects which have contributed to this investment, the Concert Hall, represents an outstanding example of the power of public, private and European partnership in Manchester. As both an international music and entertainment landmark, and as a catalyst for local regeneration, it will be the single biggest project to be completed during CMDC's lifetime and, therefore, a lasting record of the work of the Development Corporation.

In the Whitworth Street area, many of the great

listed warehouses and sites were ripe for conversion and redevelopment. CMDC rejected speculative office schemes and instead earmarked the area for residential use. The result is the 'village in the city' of more than 1,000 homes, serviced by pubs, bars, restaurants, taxi firms, Post Office, doctor and dentist and even a 24-hour shop. Appropriate commercial uses have been retained and encouraged, while striking improvements to the environment have stimulated leisure projects in what has also become an integral part of Manchester's youth and music culture.

Piccadilly Village now provides new housing units at the heart of the Regional Centre.

CMDC has also played an important role in supporting wider initiatives that promote Manchester as a whole, recognising that these benefit every part of the City. Examples here are the Manchester Olympic Bid for the Games of 2000, the Commonwealth Games Bid for 2002 and the campaign to achieve a second runway at Manchester Airport. During its lifetime CMDC has been an effective active player in the life of the City and not just a patch-based agency corporation will be disbanded at the end of March 1996 and planning powers for the designated area will revert to the City Council.

Castle Quay, a Grade 2 listed building, before refurbishment.

Castle Quay following its conversion to 44 luxury residential apartments.

The impressive bridge link between Terminal 1 and the new British Rail Station at Manchester Airport.

The heart of Chinatown, formally a run down area of warehousing now plays host to one of the largest Chinese communities in the Country.

19 Transport and Communications

The early chapters of this book highlight the impact of good transport links, notably canals and railways, both of which were vital components in promoting the City's rapid growth during the Industrial Revolution. At the present time, road, rail and air communications all help to sustain Manchester as a thriving commercial and industrial centre.

The world's first passenger railway station was opened in Manchester and the Victorians developed a network of railways serving the City, primarily for freight and commerce, but increasingly as a way of bringing people to work in the City from the expanding suburbs. Perhaps above everything else, the City has maintained its accessibility both locally and within the rest of the world, typified by developments such as the Manchester Ship Canal, Manchester Airport and, more recently, Metrolink.

Transport has also had an important influence on the physical development of the City and since the Second World War, the motor car has fundamentally changed the way in which the City works. As early as the 1920's expansion of the City took place alongside major roadways such as Kingsway and Princess Road. They were laid out as dual carriageways with tramways running down central reservations. These were accompanied by plans to widen highways along many of the older roads into the City Centre to accommodate more traffic, but in the event many were never implemented.

Below: The construction of Mancunian Way in 1966. The picture shows the widescale demolition work required to accommodate Britain's first urban motorway.

Opposite: A Metrolink tram at GMex station. The Metrolink system extends from Bury to Altrincham with City Centre links and is hugely successful.

The 1945 Plan picked up on these earlier proposals and identified a series of schemes designed to create a spider's web of ring roads and radial roads around and into the City Centre. The developments that took place in the 1950's took these proposals into account with provision for the future upgrading (normally in the form of widening) of the highway network. The 1961 Development Plan included broadly similar road proposals although on a slightly differing scale with the inclusion of a road running on a deck over the River Irwell. In 1962 the South East Lancashire and North East Cheshire (SELNEC) Highway Plan highlighted the enormous impact of ever increasing traffic volumes and endorsed the road proposals contained in the 1961 Plan. It also included schemes designed to take longer

distance through-traffic out of the urban area. New roads such as the Northenden and Sharston By-Passes (M63) were built and eventually developed to form part of the Manchester Outer Ring Road, the last section of which, between Heaton Park and Denton, is currently under construction.

A start was also made on tackling the City Centre which presented special problems. A new road was proposed to link the East Manchester radial routes with Chester Road and Regent Road to provide access to Trafford Park and the Docks area. Known first as Route 17/7 it was to become Mancunian Way, the Country's first Urban Motorway. Today the Mancunian Way forms part of the Inner Relief Route.

Priority for buses and cyclists on Oxford Road.

For functional, practical and environmental reasons, the route of the City Centre Road proposed in the 1962 SELNEC Plan was amended in the 1968 Plan. The structural deck over the Irwell was to be replaced by a new section that ran through Salford to the west of Exchange Station and linked up with the line of the Inner Relief Road north of Great Ancoats Street.

Again these proposals proved to be too costly to implement and between 1974 and 1986 the Greater Manchester Council reviewed all large scale inner City road proposals. Many were formally abolished and others replaced by more modest proposals, resulting in the lifting of blight from many thousands of properties and releasing land for redevelopment.

Despite this emphasis on road construction it has been recognised for many years that for the City to prosper it would have to have a modern efficient public transport system. The City's rail

network had long suffered from the problem that the north and south rail networks were developed by different companies and were not linked together.

The establishment of a Passenger Transport Authority for the Greater Manchester area (the SELNEC PTA) in 1968 led to proposals for an underground rail link between Manchester Piccadilly and Manchester Victoria stations. Construction of the Picc-Vic Tunnel, as it was to be known, was scheduled to begin in 1973 with completion by 1978. Considerable preparation work was undertaken on this proposal including the acquisition of property and construction sites, experimental underground tunnels and shafts. However, the funding for the project was never secured and the scheme was abandoned.

Attention then turned to what could be done to improve access for more local trips. As early as 1967 a feasibility study had been commissioned for a new rapid transit monorail system extending from Manchester Airport and Wythenshawe in the south to Middleton (Langley) in the north. The new route would have run through the Central Area and the Higher Education Precinct and enabled connections to be made between the major main line stations in the City Centre. This project was never developed.

However, following the abandonment of the Picc-Vic tunnel, attention returned to the idea of light rail. A study undertaken by Greater Manchester Council, British Rail and the Greater Manchester Passenger Transport Executive (GMPTE) in 1984 recommended that a light rapid transit system be established between Bury and Altrincham with City Centre links. Prior to its abolition the GMC promoted the necessary Parliamentary Bills to allow for its Commencement. Three years later, in 1987, the public were given a taste of the new

service when a light rail vehicle operated for three weeks on a stretch of lightly-used freight line, attracting many visitors and VIPs.

Construction of the Metrolink system began in 1991 with the closure of the British Rail services to Bury and Altrincham. The network was eventually opened in phases during 1992 with the Bury line introduced on 6 April, the Altrincham line on 15 June and the branch to Piccadilly Station on 20 July. This has proved to be a great success.

Plans for the expansion of the Metrolink system are already under way and the next phase is likely to be the line to Eccles via Salford Quays. Other possible developments include a new line via Wythenshawe to the Airport; a line to Rochdale via Oldham; a line to Ashton-under-Lyne via the Eastlands area; and a branch to East Didsbury.

Manchester Airport's second passenger Terminal (T2) which was opened in 1993 to accommodate the ever-increasing number of travellers.

The GMC used its wide revenue raising powers to heavily subsidise public transport to keep bus fares at lower levels and maintain the local British Rail commuter rail network. It also used Capital monies to invest in new suburban rail stations, electrification schemes and track rationalisation to better serve and enhance Manchester as the Regional Centre.

Links with the rest of the world are also important to the City. One hundred years ago the Manchester Ship Canal brought ocean-going vessels right into the heart of the City linking Manchester with its worldwide commercial markets. The growth in the size of ships means that this is no longer possible and the City's links with the world are now provided by the Airport.

It was back in 1919 that two Manchester men, Captain John Alcock and Lieutenant Arthur Brown, made the first non-stop flight across the Atlantic, so it is entirely fitting that the City of Manchester obtained the very first licence in Britain authorising the City Council to provide and control a municipal airport.

The new airfield was located at Rackhouse Park, Wythenshawe on the south side of Manchester, but this site was quickly superseded by a larger field at Barton to the west of the City. In 1938 the airport was re-sited at Ringway because the Barton airfield was too small for major expansion. World War II put a stop to many of the major developments planned by Manchester Corporation at the time and, during the war, Ringway became the main training centre for Allied paratroops.

The first post-war international service was introduced in June 1946 and after that date the airport expanded at a remarkable rate. A massive reconstruction programme began in 1957, and in 1962 a new terminal building was opened by HRH the Duke of Edinburgh who described the airport as 'the gateway to the world from the industrial heart of Britain.'

Since that date the airport has continued to expand. In 1984 Manchester City Council produced the Ringway Local Plan which defined an area to be reserved for airport expansion and determined how land between the airport and Wythenshawe should be developed. Expansion continued throughout the 1980s with plans for the construction of a second passenger terminal to meet the increasing throughput of passengers. The new terminal (T2) was opened in March 1993. It was complemented by the completion of a new rail link with its futuristic station, opened in May of the same year, to provide good quality public transport links both to the City Centre and the whole of the North West Region and beyond. A southern spur to the rail system to link the Airport with the Midlands and South of the country has now been established. Proposals for the creation of a second runway have been put forward recently to handle the predicted growth in air traffic movement and are strongly supported by the City Council. A major public inquiry has taken place but as yet the future of this project is undecided.

Manchester has also witnessed major advances in telecommunications. From the invention of the first computer at Manchester University in the 1940's the City's telecommunications network has grown to become as advanced as any in Britain. Manchester has been one of the first centres in the UK to benefit from the latest innovations in technology. It is the home of the first public access computer information system, the Manchester Host, developed by the City Council and backed by European Union funding. Also, Nynex is in the process of developing a new information superhighway to provide telecommunications, cable television and other multi-media services to one and a half million homes and 90,000 businesses throughout the region.

20 *The 1995 Manchester Plan*

1995 saw the adoption of the new Manchester Plan, officially known as the Unitary Development Plan. The first part of the Plan sets out the Council's strategic vision for Manchester and provides a guide to development in order to achieve wider community objectives. The second part indicates how these strategic policies apply at the local level.

The need for the Plan arose when new arrangements for development plans were put in place by the Government in 1986 (see chapter 10). These required the preparation of a Unitary Development Plan to take over from the former Greater Manchester County Structure Plan and various Local Plans.

The Plan has two broad aims. Firstly, to improve the City as a place to live, work and visit. Secondly, to sustain and revitalise the local economy. There are six major topic areas and these are summarised below.

Housing

The Council has two main aims in relation to housing. The first is to maintain and, where necessary, improve the quality of existing homes and residential areas. The second is to make use of the many opportunities to provide new housing in order to meet the needs of people who wish to live in the City and extend the range of housing available.

New housing developments in the City Centre provide evidence that city living is becoming more desirable. They are a reflection of population trends as well as changing lifestyles. Average household size is expected to fall over the next 10 to 20 years and the greatest demand will

Manchester aims for a 24 hour City at Manto Bar.

be for single person accommodation. Fortunately, there are tremendous opportunities to provide more new housing in Manchester to meet this need, particularly through the conversion of older buildings in the City Centre and new schemes on redevelopment sites throughout the rest of the City. If people can live closer to where they work and closer to shops and leisure facilities, it will reduce the need to travel. However, in order for all of this to be successful it must be accompanied by widespread measures to make the City an attractive place in which to live.

Economic Development

After a period when its economic future was uncertain, Manchester is re-emerging as an international city – a player on the world stage. The City Council wishes to see Manchester plugged in to the network of world cities which are developing as centres of decision-making, information exchange, professional services, financial institutions, research, the media, culture and sport. This will bring with it benefits for people living in the City in terms of new jobs and facilities. It will also benefit the North West Region as a whole, of which Manchester is the capital.

For the future, Manchester has a number of strengths on which to build:

- the City Centre with its concentration of facilities and attractions and its role as a centre for business, finance, shopping, leisure, tourism, culture, public services and government.

- Manchester Airport – the fastest growing in Europe.

- the concentration of media industries.

- the presence of major electronic companies.

- the Higher Education Precinct – the largest in Europe.

- the City's role as the regional centre for youth culture.

An artist's impression of the Great Bridgewater Office Development to be constructed on Lower Mosley Street next to the Bridgewater Hall and GMex.

- the Olympic and Commonwealth Games bids which have not only brought world class sporting facilities to Manchester and the region but have also placed it firmly on the map alongside other international cities.

Environmental Improvement and Protection

The City Council will be taking practical steps to protect and improve the environment. It is based on two perspectives. The first is concerned with improving the local environment for the benefit

of people who live in Manchester and people who use the City. The second is to do with the contribution that action in Manchester can make, however limited, to the solution of global environmental problems. For instance, reducing levels of air pollution caused by motor vehicles will improve air quality for local residents andmake a contribution towards controlling global greenhouse gas emissions. Similarly, reducing the number of cars in the City Centre core not only reduces pollution levels but provides the opportunity to create better conditions for pedestrians.

A major new strategy is proposed for the development of an extensive network of linear recreational routes by linking and making better use of river valleys, canals, disused railways and other areas of open space. This will open up many new areas for informal recreation and provide attractive off-road routes for pedestrians and cyclists.

Shopping

The City Council wishes to sustain Manchester as the regional shopping centre offering variety and choice for both general and specialist shoppers. This role is part and parcel of the wider regional role that Manchester plays. The Council will continue to enhance the environment of the City Centre, in particular, improving conditions for pedestrians by making it safer and cleaner. Reducing the impact of traffic is a key objective. Therefore the Council will seek to enhance public transport links to the City Centre both to ensure that it remains accessible to people who do not have access to a car and to provide a more environmentally friendly alternative for those who do.

The Council is committed to maintaining and enhancing district shopping centres so that they remain the focus for the provision of shopping facilities as well as a full range of community facilities. The Council wishes to see these centres continuing to benefit from investment and, where necessary, renewal.

Throughout the City, the Council wishes to ensure that good quality, local and convenient shopping facilities are within easy reach of people's homes.

Leisure

The City's population is changing both in overall size and social composition. These changes have important implications for active recreation. Quantity, quality and accessibility are all important considerations in terms of future leisure provision.

The City Council wishes to see the development of a wide range of indoor and outdoor leisure facilities which meet the needs of the City's residents. Some of these facilities will be of a very high standard, recognising Manchester's status as a major European city which plays host to events of international importance. Leisure developments need to provide for multi-purpose use in order to maximise their value to local communities.

One of the major issues facing the Council is to find resources to maintain and improve the quality of the City's parks and recreation areas. The approach the Council is taking involves increasing recreational opportunities in some of the larger sites such as Heaton Park and Wythenshawe Park consistent with their primary role as parks. The benefits will be access to more leisure facilities, with more people using the parks making them safer, and generating resources for the maintenance and enhancement of all recreational areas.

The successful bid to become Britain's City of Drama in 1994 and the construction of the Bridgewater Hall, a new home for the City's orchestras, illustrate the importance of Manchester as a cultural centre. The City Council is a major player in such initiatives and strongly supports the development of the City as a centre for the arts and culture.

Transport

The City Council wishes to ensure that Manchester enjoys the benefits of a transport system equal to the best in Europe. It sees the development of such a system, and the high level of accessibility it would provide, as vital to the future economic well-being of the City. An improved transport system will play a major part in Manchester developing as a cosmopolitan and international city able to attract investment, activity and visitors from around the world. The further development of the Airport is seen as a vital element of this strategy.

The overall environment of the City will be improved if public transport plays a larger part in meeting future travel needs. It will reduce pollution, cut accidents and save energy. The Metrolink tram system is evidence of the successful promotion of public transport and the Council fully supports expansion of the network.

In addition, the plan sets out policies to improve accessibility for a large number of people. Much has already been achieved in terms of incorporating facilities for disabled people in major new schemes such as the Manchester Arena and the Concert Hall. Relatively small scale measures will be encouraged such as improvements to pavement surfaces, better provision for cyclists and access improvements for disabled people. Collectively, such initiatives can have a significant impact.

In the aftermath of World War II, the 1945 Plan presented a vision for regeneration and renewal. Fifty years on, the new plan for Manchester sets out a fresh agenda to guide development into the next century.

21 The Environment and Sustainability

After World War II the priority in Manchester was to deal with bomb damage and the problems inherited from the Industrial Revolution. At that time, the aim was to achieve environmental improvement through renewal. Open space and clean air were acknowledged as essential requirements for a healthy urban population. Manchester was the first local authority in Britain to introduce smoke emission restrictions in 1953.

In later years, the decline of heavy industry and clearance of slum housing offered the Council, in partnership with the GMC, an opportunity to reclaim land and create green spaces along river valleys leading into the heart of the City. Planning policies drawn up during the 1970's and 1980's established green fingers in the Irk, Medlock and Mersey Valleys, providing informal recreational facilities for local residents unable to use open countryside.

Derelict land arising from the industrial closures, particularly those of the early 1980's, presented a major environmental challenge in certain parts of the City such as East Manchester (see chapter 12). Improvement work continues to bring about the re-use of these sites. For example, more than 250 acres of despoiled land was reclaimed over the five-year period between 1988 and 1993. But new derelict sites will continue to be created through the process of economic regeneration and renewal and the Council will need to engage in an ongoing programme of action to deal with the problem. Indeed, notwithstanding this very active phase of derelict land treatment, the amount of land categorised as derelict in 1993 was actually 30 per cent greater than in 1988. This shows how much of this sort of work needs to be carried out just to stand still, especially when national economic recession conditions create the circumstances that bring about dereliction.

During the 1980's the Council broadened its range of action, bringing forward new initiatives such as the cleaning of building façades, pedestrianisation schemes and new routes for cyclists.

Back in 1953, Blackley Forest became one of the country's first community based planting schemes and it pointed the way for future projects. In the 1980's tree planting and woodland creation became an important aspect of the Council's environmental agenda. River valleys were important areas of action but smaller sites were also identified in parks and schools. On average 10,000 trees were planted each year between 1986 and 1992, many as part of community projects. In 1991 the Red Rose Forest was created. It represents a network of woodland areas extending across South Lancashire and including parts of the Manchester conurbation and will help encourage further tree planting within the City.

Sustainable Development

The concept of sustainable development is not new to Manchester but the term did not achieve common usage until 1992 when the Earth Summit Conference took place in Rio de Janeiro. The conference confirmed an acceptance by most national governments that action should be taken on a

Local children learn about the importance of recycling.

wide range of environmental issues which were seen to have global consequences. In effect, this set an agenda for the twenty-first century, a plan of action more commonly referred to as Agenda 21.

From an environmental point of view, the Earth Summit acknowledged that the world's resources were finite and concluded that proposals for new developments (both large and small) should be considered carefully in terms of their immediate and long term effects. In other words, future generations should not be expected to suffer the adverse consequences of action taken today.

As well as thinking about these global perspectives, the output from the Earth Summit also included some very important guidance about local action. The slogan that was popularised was 'think global, act local', and this is as important in its own way as thinking about environmental sustainability from a world perspective. Thus, emphasis was placed on Local Agenda 21 Statements to be prepared on a shared basis by local interests, and local authorities were invited to take the lead in this process.

Two years after the Rio Conference, Manchester hosted the follow-up conference known as Global

Involving local school children in environmental issues.

Forum 94. Representatives from throughout the world met in Manchester to address areas of common concern, exchange ideas and agree a range of actions and new initiatives to translate global concerns into programmes of local action. One element of this, in which the City Council played a leading role, was a Local Authority Key Sector conference which focused on the Local Agenda 21 process and what local authorities can do to promote such action. The outputs of that conference have recently been published in collaboration between Manchester City Council and HMSO and *First Steps* consists of a series of case studies from throughout the world about Local Agenda 21 in action.

In Manchester over recent years there has been a progressive increase in efforts to understand the implications of sustainability in modern city planning. Traditional issues such as land use and transportation planning have been broadened to incorporate environmental concerns such as pollution, waste management, energy conservation and mobility. In this way it is now possible to consider social, economic and environmental matters together. The Council established a Local Agenda 21 Forum forming a partnership between public, private and voluntary interests within the City. Collectively, they have begun the process of drawing up an overall strategy of action.

The Council began this process by committing itself in Autumn 1993 to approximately 100 changes (known as the Manchester 100) that it could make itself, or could promote, which would contribute to making Manchester a more sustainable city. More recently, an environmental checklist has been introduced for use with planning applications. The leaflet invites developers to consider a range of environmental concerns before submitting their proposals for approval. Within the new Plan for Manchester (see chapter 20) the Council expresses its commitment to controlling air pollution, improving water quality, protecting wildlife and Sites of Biological Importance. Elsewhere, a campaign for recycling of waste has been launched and the Council is seeking to introduce energy saving measures through its stock of municipal housing.

A strategy for sustainable development in Manchester involves issues that were not fully appreciated 50 years ago but the benefits of earlier environmental policies are now apparent: industrial and domestic air pollution created by coal fires is a thing of the past; derelict land in the inner city has been reclaimed; old buildings have been refurbished; rivers and canals are cleaner and greener; tens of thousands of trees have been planted; new cycleways have been created and passenger miles on routes covered by Metrolink have tripled in just 3 years.

The most important lesson learnt over the past 50 years has been the need to consult and involve local people in decision-making. Developing a sense of ownership and responsibility in the care of the environment needs to be fostered wherever possible. The concept of sustainable development however, has received only limited acceptance and the global implications of local actions are not always fully understood. Much work remains to be done to raise awareness and change attitudes across all sections of the community. We need to protect what we have and develop new policies to tackle broad environmental concerns in order to improve the quality of life for future generations.

22 Manchester City Development Guide

As one of the first cities to experience the effects of the Industrial Revolution, Manchester was not a particularly pleasant place 150 or so years ago. It was dirty, overcrowded, unhealthy and most of its people lived and worked in seemingly intolerable conditions. Much of the history of planning in Manchester is a story of attempts to tackle these evils (see chapters 1–5).

Improved housing, industrial zoning, road building and environmental improvements have transformed the congested urban area into a modern city. However, during this process of change,

mistakes have been made and it is important that the diversity and character which makes great cities work be reintroduced into Manchester's urban fabric in those parts of the City where it has been lost. The Draft Manchester City Development Guide is an attempt to help with this process.

The first opportunity to implement these ideas was the 1990's redevelopment of Hulme (see chapter 9). It was therefore in Hulme that Manchester's new urban vision has been given form. The Hulme Guide to Development, published in June 1994, both explained the urban vision and set out a series of simple rules based on this thinking and upon analysis of the characteristics of traditional successful urban form.

The Draft City Development Guide emerged from the Hulme experience. In Hulme the

An example of good street design in Denmark.

STRETFORD ROAD GATEWAY

An artist's impression of the proposed Stretford Road Gateway, part of the Hulme regeneration strategy.

Council had wide-ranging powers. It owned the land and controlled the allocation of financial resources as well as being the planning and highways authority. This allowed the Hulme Guide to go beyond that which would usually be regarded as achievable through normal planning controls. Many of the people involved in the process of assimilating the Hulme Guide became convinced that its principles should be applied more widely across the City, whilst recognising that circumstances throughout the City were very different to those found in Hulme.

To achieve this an Advisory Panel was established to draw up a development guide for the whole City. The panel included architects, surveyors, engineers, planners and academics and was first convened in the early autumn of 1994. Following a consultation process and a series of case studies the Panel produced a Draft City Development Guide for further consultation in June 1995.

The Draft City Development Guide remained largely faithful to the Hulme Guide in its format and content. A new section was added on safety and security and a greater emphasis was placed on the quality of development. It also sought to widen the range of development covered and included a City Centre section. Some of its provisions were more flexible than the Hulme Guide, acknowledging the need to relate its principles to the diverse range of urban forms which make up the City of Manchester.

The main elements of the City Guide are:

- A Hierarchy of Streets – At the core of the Guide is the street. A hierarchy of streets is set out from major roads to high streets with different rules applying to each. All buildings are to face onto and enclose these streets to create the public face of the City.

- Density, Integration and a Mix of Uses – The Guide specifies that where possible streets should contain a mix of uses and development should not be zoned into separate housing, business or industrial estates. It also recommends that housing and other uses should be built to higher densities than has generally been the case in recent years.

- Permeability – This process requires that streets should link to other streets and, for example, encourage through movement so that cul-de-sacs are avoided.

- Transport and Car Parking – Here the Guide proposes a more traditional approach. In particular it seeks to promote crossroads, reduce dimensions of corners and does not specify minimum parking requirements.

- Landmarks, Vistas and Focal Points – The Guide requires that all developers should consider the contribution that their scheme can make to the City's townscape. This might include the emphasis of corner features, the retention of historic buildings and the use of public art.

- Quality Space – One of the most important recommendations is that buildings respect a clear building line and are scaled in proportion to the street to ensure that public space is clearly defined, enclosed and well proportioned.

- Identity – The Guide seeks to encourage quality design and architectural expression to create buildings of good proportion and strong identity.

- Security – The Guide recommends that attention should be paid to minimising the impact of crime. For example, buildings should not be hidden from view behind security barriers such as high walls. Ideally they should provide surrounding streets with natural surveillance thereby making them safer.

- Environmental Sustainability – The Guide suggests that higher density, mixed development is more sustainable since it promotes public transport and reduces car use. The guide proposes that trees are retained and planted, that natural habitats are protected, that segregated waste collection is implemented and that buildings are energy efficient.

At the time of writing, wide-ranging public consultations have been completed and discussions about the final shape of the Guide are underway. However, it is clear that a momentum towards a new approach to urban design has been established.

Photographic Acknowledgements

Central Library
Burnage Garden Village
Victoria Court
Air Raids
Miller Street
Cannon Street
Parker Street
Civic Centre Proposed
Wythenshawe Civic Centre
Miles Platting
Maths Tower
Hattersley
Watts Warehouse
Building of Manchester Ship Canal
Victorian Sketch Manchester

Jefferson's
Concert Hall
Nynex Arena
Aerial Manchester Town Centre
Aerial Manchester Education Precinct
Aerial Hulme Crescents
Velodrome
Airport Railway

Chris Makepeace
Victorian Scene
Slums Redbank
Free Trade Hall

P & O Property Services
Arndale Centre

Marketing Manchester
Manto Cafe Bar

Hulme Regeneration Limited
Demolishing of Crescents
New build in Hulme
Stretford Gateway

Bridget Soltau
Hulme Consultations*

Paul Herrmann
Hulme Crescents*

Manchester City Council Special Projects
Eastlands Site
Millennium Stadium

Len Grant
St Ann's Square on Cover & in Chapter

Stephenson Architecture
15 Quay Street
Trinity Court Interior

George Mills Architects
Offices, Peter Street
Metropolitan University

Buttress, Fuller, Alsop
Offices, 37 King Street

Holford Associates
81 Fountain Street

Central Manchester Development Corporation
Eastgate before
Eastgate after
Piccadilly before
Piccadilly after
Castle Quay before
Castle Quay after
Bridgewater Offices

Margaret Robinson
Bus lane
Tram at GMex

*Author and publisher have attempted, so far without success, to trace the copyright holder for the Hulme Consultations and Hulme Crescents photographs (by Bridget Soltau and Paul Herrmann respectively), which appear in chapter 9. If the legal copyright holders in question wish to contact HMSO, we shall ensure that the correct acknowledgement appears in any future edition of this book.

Printed in the United Kingdom for HMSO
Dd 301377   11/95   C10   Ord